CARMELITE MONASTERY
LIBRARY
SARANAC LAKE, N Y

# The Words Our Savior Gave Us

# The Words Our Savior Gave Us

Daniel Berrigan

CARMELITE MONASTERY
LIBRARY
SARANAC LAKE, N Y

TEMPLEGATE PUBLISHERS
Springfield, Illinois

242.51

© 1978 by Daniel Berrigan

All rights reserved, including
the right of reproduction in whole or
in part, in any form.

Published by
TEMPLEGATE PUBLISHERS
302 East Adams Street, P.O. Box 963
Springfield, Illinois 62705

ISBN 87243-081-2

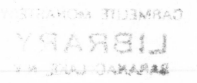

# Contents

Our Father........................................11

You Who Are in Heaven............................31

Hallowed Be Your Name............................45

Your Kingdom Come................................59

Your Will Be Done on
Earth as It Is in Heaven.........................73

Give Us This Day Our Daily Bread....................83

Forgive the Wrongs We Have
Committed, as We Forgive the
Wrongs We Have Done to Others.....................97

And Lead Us Not Into
Temptation but Deliver Us From Evil................111

An Afterword.....................................121

## Our Father

Matthew opens his gospel with a genealogy of Christ. A highly selective one; we might not be far from the mark to say, a "metaphorical" one.

"This is the bloodline of Jesus Christ, son of Abraham, son of David."

He places Jesus in the long uninterrupted line of those who believed. This is said proudly, almost easily; though in fact we know at least in measure what the faith has cost those who were faithful.

But it must also be remembered that Jesus stood in the line of those who sinned. The line of David, the sinner par excellence.

Matthew, in this brief account of a family history, wishes to underscore only two, out of a possible hundred or more, ancestors of the Lord. The one who will speak familiarly of "My father", and then invite us into the circle of friendship, "When you pray, say; Our Father . . ." — this self declared friend and brother, is also inviting us to look at another side of things. At another side of himself.

As to this human side, it is worth noting also, at the outset, that "the family" never seemed to be of great moment to him. He tended to put it down; it smacked too nearly of tribalism and pride, and He had other business in the world than to glorify that dark call of the blood. "Couldn't God raise up sons of Abraham from the stones of the road?" The tone of John echoed his own; it was mocking, down-putting.

Jesus indeed set up oppositions, where the state, human reason, affection, sound morality, religion even, would counsel otherwise. "Leave father and mother and come follow me . . ." It was unsettling in the extreme, then as now.

So there was that side of things: family, genealogy, signs and sounds of recognition, marriage and human love, care of children, the whole subtle strong web that binds us, holds us in place, tells us in a thousand colorations of tone and glance who we are, gives reason and sense and continuity to existence. A web that sometimes also enslaves us.

And that was the rub. It rubbed the soul raw.

We might be inclined to think we don't need a savior to tell us that the family, as presently set up and functioning, is often a stalking horror to those born into it, or married into it — or dying in it. Perhaps. Perhaps a mere observation is enough to set people in pursuit of something better, more human.

Perhaps. And then again, perhaps not. Is something more needed, for a fresh start? One is tempted to point out in this regard that the cultures that seem to fall hardest are precisely those which, on a modern scale, would rate the encomium "developed." And that within such cultures, there is never lacking a bewildering variety of learned voices, skills, research, all assuring one that (for example) the family or the law courts, or the jails, or the churches, or the universities are in need of heavy overhaul.

After which nothing occurs. Except that the scholastic game goes on. And the power of initiating change, real change, modest, pro human change, languishes, withers away . . .

This unpleasant discussion is all but done. It was undertaken only by way of suggesting that we take a long look at another method of considering human life, than the academic. Another way, which I would make bold to suggest is the method of Jesus.

I will call it, for want of a better term, the metaphorical method. It proceeds, as we read the gospel, by way of three stages: first an invitation or analogy; then, unexpectedly (and many would say, unfairly) a conflict enters, an irony, a crashing opposition. And finally (this does not always occur, sometimes we are merely left hanging) he fuses that initial metaphor, under pressure, stress, dread, under violence overcome, under a furious application of ice and fire; under death. And this is the moment of truth; and of course it first sounded in his own life. Much more than in his words — though in his case the words are transparent, an epiphany of life itself. Also since his words are set down, it seems clear they are meant to be extemporized on, improvised by ourselves. ("When you pray, say . . . ")

Take the metaphor of "father", one quite dear to him, and firmly present in all four gospels. First of all, let us consider the metaphor as thought through, applied, put to his own case. "My father." The figure seems at first glance to imply no discomfort, no friction. Why should it? His human genealogy was a bloodline like our own. Then he points to something different — his father is "heavenly", not of this world, not of our flesh. Shall we call this a bloodline of the spirit?

Well, we think, whatever we call it, at least it offers some relief from the human! Perhaps Jesus opens this part of his existence, to remind us that he and we have an escape hatch from precisely those terrors, that fate, which human birth opens, like a hideous Pandora's box terrorizing an infant.

We're stuck with this world, let us face up to it — but at least there's another one! If we must cope — with one another, with neutron bombs, with the snarling absurdity of our nightmares and daymares — at least there's a Father, God, a Solution, an extraterrestrial deity, a ground of being somewhere, somewhere under the Big Fault . . . Oh we have names for it, him, her, them!

The only trouble is there is absolutely no truth to all this. There is no such god, at least according to Jesus. That there is such a god, according to the world, according to America, according to the Pentagon, according to the culturally convening churches and synagogues — according to our own

13

dreads and day dreams and unexorcised demons — this should not detain us beyond measure, since by agreement we are meditating the God according to Jesus.

And Jesus leads us inexorably to a second degree of understanding. Into deeper waters. You see, if he is born into the world, in our bloodline, if he dies on our tree, then it is God who does these things, the Father who permits these things. We must speak of cancer and early death and the inflated victory of evil power, and hunger and poverty and spiritual degradation (among rich and poor) in this world, in this time, now, here. With such a God are we stuck. Indeed, as Jesus sternly reminds us, we are to adore no other.

The God who hurts, and who hurts us. A law of pain in the world. A son who sweats it out, in blood. "My father, if it be possible let this cup pass . . . " What crueler evidence than the events of the vicious, chaotic, uncontrollable hours that follow on his cry — what crueler evidence that relief was not possible, that the chalice did not pass from his lips, but was drained to the lees, even as his body was drained?

We are in the midst of the oppositions, ironies, which that phrase "My father" (our father also) introduces.

He is not to have it easy, he is not a Son at the end of a golden umbilical, at the Other End of which stands the Platonic Solutionizer, saying, "My son, you may, by some crude whimsy of your own, decide to depart from these Crystalline Headquarters for a time. I will even allow that; there is certain whimsical interest in tasting the vagaries, the cruelty, the black humors of this recalcitrant tribe, with which long ago I signed (and what a relief!) a nonintervention pact. I wanted nothing more for my part than a hands-off policy, and for theirs, an end to my command appearance at their rites, their complaints, their dreads, their insolvent lives. Now, at least, I know a measure of peace. Still, you wish to visit them. To observe their customs, note their observances. Analogies occur: Gulliver among the Lilliputians. May I suggest that as a safety precaution, you tie this invisible golden thread to your left ankle; the other end I shall attach loosely to the left foot of a bird of paradise in our garden. On occasion of crisis, capture or threat, you have only to twitch your ankle three times; the bird will scream, and twelve squads of angels will be dispatched to your aid . . . ''

No it was not like that. We do not know why that cup had necessarily to be drunk, but to admit our ignorance is by no means to rush into false judgement. At least we know this: there was no life line. There was no hasty exit from death, no safety hatch. Jesus went through it all, that blood and terror. Then, and only then, the Father raised Him up. Then the father showed himself for what he was, in power, as the son had shown himself for what he was, in obedience. And this is the third stage of knowledge: experience. He learned compassion by the things he endured, Paul says.

Perhaps we can think of the metaphor of "father" as it touches ourselves. Apparently this is the intention of Jesus; that we enter the act — or better, the series of acts which brought him literally to a new plane of existence. First the metaphor ("our Father") — rather unexamined, for the most part, one of those phrases that pass easily over the tongue. But we are not being invited to twitch a golden thread, in view of an instant recourse. Let us look a little more in detail at what we are called to.

The first political act of anyone is simply getting born. Look at the fact of genetic tampering, or abortion. The depleted earth, so cut off from mystical identity with its dwellers, is looked on today somewhat like a thanksgiving turkey on the hoof — delectable indeed, but only so much meat, and therefore fenced off and guarded by the "owners." Unwanted births must be curtailed (along with the disposal of the aged, the unachieving, the political deviants.)

The sword point of the empire is pressed against the womb. We might not have expected the Herod event to be a rather consistent mode of acting, when the empire is threatened by an interloper. But already, so soon after the birth of Jesus, we pass from the easy phrase "our Father", as well as the assumed ease of the phrase as it formed on his lips, "My father." How quickly we are done with easy phrases, when the conduct of God is our concern! When God (or the godlike) enter upon the scene, they need do no more; trouble erupts from the throne.

So small a space did he claim in the world, so little of its air and light and heat! His claim, his serious truth, could not, at first, even be formulated by his own mouth. How shall the newborn infant call out the name of his Father? What threat would such a claim imply?

We do well not to underestimate Herod. He knows in his imperial bones that a genuinely religious claim is an immediate political threat. The child need not utter the claim; his existence is his crime. (And in any case, God has a thousand ways of letting the truth be known. If the children are silent, will not the stones cry out?)

More than stones, in this instance. The wise men read the signs, inklings, clues, and come in haste. They are blessedly naive. They do not know the biblical scepticism about imperial virtue, they know only the stars. They dream of a virtuous king, who would welcome and honor the "king of the Jews." So, all unwittingly, their simplicity does a terrible thing; it unsheathes the king's sword.

And inevitably Herod understands. He understands the threat, in an acute fashion that is like the dark side of the self understanding of Jesus himself. Herod knows the future, he reads the mortal danger to the kingdom of this world, implicit in the birth of the King whose kingdom "is not of this world."

Jesus is of this world and he is not of this world. He is "son of David, son of Abraham." He is also son of the most high. Indeed, if he were only from here, or only from there, he could the more easily be dealt with. But he is from both, and the future is a cloud of contention, as Herod sees. Conflict is inevitable. Life and death will clash. The method of God — which is all-creative, favoring life, nurturing the victims, healing, restoring, uniting, reconciling, raising the very dead — must encounter another method, the method of this world, which is the imperial method. A method that is indeed implicit in the conduct of earthly power and authority: in all that diminishes, discourages, wounds, punishes, rejects, tortures, interrogates, locks up, executes, or summarily murders. But these methods are ordinarily dissipated throughout the world in a myriad network of nations and cultures and families and structures. And there they are mitigated to a degree, weakened by humanity, sentiment, love, compassion, justice even. But in the full blown imperial entity, here named Herod (elsewhere in the Bible called Pharaoh, Babylon, Assyria, Rome) the method of death exists in its pure, naked, inexorable state. Herod unsheathes his sword. A stunning instance, by no means the first or the last, of a "definitive solution."

But let us also mediate on the "crime" of the newborn, a crime which exacted so hysterical and inflated a reaction. Understanding the "crime" of the newborn Jesus is crucial to all religious understanding that is not bogged down in quietism, the long sleep of the late '70's.

The crime? Being God. Being godlike. Standing for life. Standing against death, by whomever purveyed, huckstered, decreed. Asserting the claim of a higher existence, superior to the power that (today or in ancient times) declares war, condemns accused persons to capital punishment, enforces systems of economic or chattel slavery, maintains spies, politicizes police forces, glorifies or condones or is silent before the denial of human rights, stockpiles nuclear weapons (we are now uncomfortably close to home), exalts property as a value superior to human life, amasses great fortunes, encourages or finances or validates production of ever more destructive devices of war. This is to be resisted. This conduct God resists. The child Emmanuel, God resisting the empire of death, and its king.

Where death has been the ordinary method all along, under crisis it will become a truly abundant, generous method, a useful metaphor expands, a hyperbole. Let much blood flow, let many children be destroyed, to ensure that the one who must be destroyed is once and for all disposed of. This child

17

must not be allowed to say, "My Father", to invite the world to say "our Father." That he is too young to shape the words, let alone to instruct others, is hardly the point. His birth is his crime. The presence of such a god in the community of citizens, of good, silent, enlisted, tax paying, acquiescent, lock-stepping citizens for the large part (then as now), among them, this presence is the crime. This dissident god, this raiser of questions, this non-cog in the imperial machinery, this one whom no threats will silence nor bribes win over, this one who cannot be absorbed into religion or real politik, this one who will blaspheme and raise large claims and disturb the right order, the impervious law, with his brusque interfering hands — crucify him!

The sword of Herod would prevent all that later turmoil; a pre-emptive strike, so to speak.

Whence it would seem to follow

— We cannot say "our Father" with anything near all our heart, or with an undivided mind, and still endorse the method and ideology of death.

That statement is perhaps, in the manner of most religious teaching today, too abstract to have bite. But its conclusions, for those who have the courage to pursue them, are momentous, costly, and commonly neglected.

The stocking of nuclear arms is a simple naked translation of the unsheathing of Herod's sword. But today the sword, in a supreme irony, is in Christian hands, tightly held, ominous, just short of being wielded. The sword has even been blessed, with that silent blessing of acquiescence, an immemorial Christian rite and skill. And when it begins its downward arc, cutting a universal swath, it will be because some virtuous madman, in full possession of his ego, his authority, his Christian faith, will have concluded that it is for the good of humanity that humanity be liquidated.

Our Father indeed. It is quite possible that such words arise to the lips of the murderer of humanity, that in the name of the God of life, he out-Herods Herod.

Somber reflections. But however crude or intemperate (and

18

I believe they are neither, but stark fact) they have this virtue: they peel away from mad authority (Herod's, today's) that baleful aura that keeps sanity at a distance, prevents access and understanding, deifies those in high places, accords them a quasi-divine access to the "facts", to secret truths, even to God's will. Such mystical nonsense creates a phalanx of mercenary citizens around Herod — humanoids, enlisters, moral dwarfs, inventive killers. No, we must look cooly, free of mystification, at the human heart, however highly placed — or however lowly, even at the heart in hell.

We would like, with all our coward hearts, to be able to say "our Father", and still dwell at peace in the kingdom of disarray, the kingdom of necessity. For those who dream of so sublime an arrangement, the infant Christ has news. So, for that matter, does Herod.

On the day of the Holy Innocents in 1978 a group of Christians splashed their own blood on the portals of the Pentagon. This shocking activity, I am told, was seen by them as a kind of liturgy, a dramatic enactment of the crime of modern Herods who have concocted, in this year of our Lord, the ineffable neutron bomb. Christian bemusement at the act was matched only by public indifference. It is as though the mothers and fathers of nations, in an orgy of abasement and blood sacrifice, were willingly, fervently holding up their infants before the nuclear blade. "Our Father!" they saluted the nuclear beast, in ecstasy.

In such dreadful circumstances as afflict us, the Lord's prayer can be seen only as a prayer of resistance. "Our Father". The arms of Jesus at prayer encircle the whole of humanity, a great ring of light and life. How shall he (or we) approach the Father except in the company of our sisters and brothers? The gesture is liturgically valid; expanding, a gesture of inclusion; then an ascension to the Father.

But how shall we pray in such a fashion, which is the way of Jesus, and still live at peace with the destruction of our people and of every people, seriously considered, dreadfully implemented by the nuclear savages? How pay a like tribute to Jesus and Herod, to the God of life and the demons of death? Truly we are witnesses of, perhaps victims of, a monstrous schism in the human soul.

My mind reverts to the crisis of German Catholics under Hitler. A fervent, well-instructed, even sophisticated body of believers — such, we are told, was the German Christian Church. Yet when Hitler's fist came down, and Christians were required to enlist in a crime of truly Herodian proportions, how few there were found to resist! "The issue" was never clear, we are told — except to a few; and those few were generally unknown, out of the public eye or high positions of authority: a Delp, a Bonhoeffer, a Jagerstatter.

To me the sorrowful and instructive point of this is not the obvious one, what we might call the nearly universal evangelical illiteracy of German Christians. Something else: the failure of a tradition. After many hundreds of years of Christianity, after the life and death of Jesus, after the great "cloud of witnesses", after sacraments multiplied, and schools and monasteries flourishing, and noble women and men by the millions living and dying under the sign of the cross — after all this, so feeble a bang, so pitiful a whimper.

But we are afflicted with the hindsight. Stalled there, in the past, unless an historic tragedy sheds some measure of light on our own dilemma. Allowing us to take with perfect seriousness the horrors of our own lifetime.

One wants to linger over those two words;
—"Our". A possessive adjective, plural, first person, we are told by the grammarians. So be it. I glance outside as I write this, a perfect lucid December day, a wedding of creation, the land looking toward the sea, the sea meeting the sky at an enchanting distance, only the dimly apprehensible line of the horizon, aerated water meeting hazy dreamy air. A stone wall meanders nearby, a long motionless underpinning, the land's serpentine rhythms. An imperfect world endlessly self-renewing, self-reliant, self-giving. Many voices, an "our" never said, never gainsaid.

Let us say that word "our."

To say it is to stand with life, for life. To stand with the God of life. To say it is to stand with one another at a time when humans, that most endangering species, are endangering one another. Public authorities today remind us of nothing so much as the stalking, bomb-carrying anarchist in Conrad's terrifying novel. They have wired humanity for its own destruction. The icy eyed protagonist of fiction is perilously close to "coming true". Lucid, inventive, mad as a March moon, he stalks about in solitude, nursing his grudges, dreaming of the terrible act that will cleanse him once and forever of the burden of existence. That will also recoup his losses, his esteem, his wounded ego. Vengeance! Justice!

We are not to think of such madness as "fetched" or moon-struck or raving. We must think of the cold sanity of inhuman power, the perfect machine-tooled machine-constructing animal, the man completely absorbed, in a demonic as well as an intellectual sense, in his machine. His guts are cold steel. His heart is icy, impermeable. His soul? Words fail.

But let us discuss his virtues, as charity demands. He undoubtedly loves his family, is monogamous, and, within his class interests and calculations, also magnanimous. To revert to the word "our" as a touchstone of consciousness, his "our" is a fist closed upon an irreduceable element, adamant, the perdurance of his system. Concerning that interest, whether it be nuclear secrets or the care and nurture of a dollar or the latest international chess move of imperial diplomacy, he is concrete as very hell. If the adamant could be rendered harder, closer, more precious, by the grasp of his fist, he would make it so. And when his eye rests on his treasure, his look is all but sub-microscopic, in intensity and detail. He sees the particles swinging in the orbit about their center (his family, his career, his government, his interests) — and he holds all these tightly, and wishes them well, and would protect them with the blood of his right hand. This is his "our"; it is unfortunately no more than a thing, a property, his: sons, daughters, wife, his flesh and blood. But you understand, still and ultimately, his. Like the limousine in the drive, or the cold meat in the freezer. For tomorrow's need, or the next meal, or convenient transport.

Everything else, everyone else, you, me, the world of the living, are abstract. Things, out there, lacking even the designing, drawing virtue of existing in here, close. Things, out there, and therefore expendable; subjects of betrayal, connivance, old-fashioned chicanery, horse swapping. City swapping. The neutron bomb — the right weapon, the unwittingly correct instrument to take the measure of the modern soul, to cut surgically through its mystery, lay bare its tegument and structure. And the bomb turns on its maker; to such a soul, the warm various lovely world of people and nations and races — all these are a simple brutal wooden "it." He is anarchic, he is anti-creation. Down with it; let it come down.

The "our" of the prayer is inclusive of the community of humankind. If it is not, it is simple mockery.

It expresses nonviolent love for all (with, of course, acknowledged differences of kin, marriage, friendship). But at the least the one who prays draws this ethical line: he/she will neither physically nor spiritually harm another human, for whatever advantage or purported gain. That line once drawn, we are free to explore the vast unknown terrain of affection, sacrifice, passionate love, unfeigned friendship with all beings.

The reality of "our" implies sacrifice. This is unpleasant material, hardly palatable today. But to speak of the modern world, modern sensibility, modern authority and its tortuous ways — to speak of ourselves — is to summon up the clear-sighted, rationally mad, icy brutalization of whole peoples, the degrading atmosphere in which minimal standards of honorable conduct toward the powerless, the poor, politically deviant, minority peoples, are daily violated as a cruel matter of course, are reported with a mad detachment, are ingested with a mad stolidity. We breathe that polluted air, since breathe we must. And to breathe polluted air seems better than virtuously to stop breathing. But whose soul is not damaged simply by existing in such a world, with eyes open? Who is not tempted to close his eyes, a contrasting mad mime, the privilege of those detached enough, or rich enough, to create their own dream world? Who is not tempted to be led about in this dream world by the hand, to receive, on the hour, the specific drug that nurtures illusion — whether its name be bland religion or civic trust in madmen?

No, we must not yield. To retain the circle of "our" is undeniably a harsh discipline and struggle. We are defending a minimal humanity — in ourselves, for the sake of others. We are at the same time humiliated at the very terms of the struggle. Who would have thought it necessary, in a sane world, to protect against an abomination like the neutron bomb?

"Our" consolation is — God. A resisting God, in Christ Jesus. Let us take that comfort to ourselves, which is indeed a cold and steely comfort, the comfort of articulated belief, the bone under flesh, that strength in virtue of which we stand upright.

Let us say the word Father. (Or Mother.)

Let us declare this further mystery, compounded with the mystery of one another, yet transcending our psychology, our skills and genius, our long bloody ambiguous history. Let us take someone's word for it: we are not condemned to be what we have been.

Let us grant too that acceptance of the word, Father, is not the easiest task we have ever undertaken. At the head of the difficulty, I think, lies the ambiguous conduct of this Father in the matter of his Son's execution. A refusal, a non-intervention. We would like to know more of that.

On the one hand, there was a cry for help: "My father, if it is possible . . . " — a cry that seemed entirely fitting; to whom else would a good son turn in his supreme hour?

But the cry went unheard, so far as we can discern. Its only recorded echo was the cry from the cross, also filial, resigned, loving, final. "Into your hands . . . "

We will never have done wondering at these two beings, one visibly present among us, the other remote, a spirit, yet always present, a presence and a pressure, like an invisible hand pressing upon one's shoulder, turning one brusquely in this direction rather than that . . .

He called himself Son; he called that other one, Father. It was the nearest human language could come; a bonding, a friendship, a genesis, mutuality, resemblance, poise and counterpoise, instructor and learner, giver and given, the hand, the eye that turns about, the one who sees and tells, the other who nods and responds. We ask for analogies to surround this too-great light. Let us walk by it. The darkness is very great.

I remember our father was a great story teller. (I am telling about "our father", the father of six sons; and I am telling a story about a supreme artist of the spoken word.) Those were times of rare relaxation. His stern face melted, he turned toward us and his tongue blossomed. He was something like the *motor mundi*, the god of the middle ages, the one who put together and then did maintenance on the vast machine of the universe. Only the one who created it, its nuts, bolts, sockets, winches, hands, gears, sprockets, quirks, nuances, moods, myriad parts within parts — only this one could be trusted to keep the wonder in motion at all.

The figure is apt because our father was a locomotive engineer and fireman, on the western prairies of the States and Canada. Whether he embroidered his tales or not was never our concern. The stories stood by themselves: weighty, adult, skilled, dangerous. "Pa, tell us a story!" "Well, let's see . . ." He'd begin with mock reluctance, someone giving away secrets that bordered on the sacred, the magical, a dredged-up store of memory, travail and triumph. Whose were they, these stories of wrongs righted, evils marvelously surmounted? That bony-faced large-handed sternly-squared wonder, he was giving himself away, we sensed it, we sensed it, we sat there silent, transfixed.

A father is someone who tells stories to children. I am willing to let pass for the moment all weighty matter of genesis, of moral demand, of the call to accountability and fidelity that sometimes creates heroes and, more often than not, brings on enmities, abject collapses, flights, terrors. We can presume all that; it is part of our dolorous history and knowledge. What is not generally thought of, I suggest, is that Jesus chose this metaphor of father and son (chose it, moreover, for us: "when you pray, use these words, Our Father . . .") because his mind was enlivened and his heart enkindled by stories that surrounded him and this other, through all time, and beyond time. How a father had a father and he a father, and so on, pushing back the history until its obscurity was relieved by that voice, that echo, another face, a figure stepping from shadow . . . And so a whole tradition was established in the only way it can be made present, urgent, inviting. A father opens the portals of history, makes sense of near or total nonsense, relieves the absurdity and horror of present existence with the gracious supple suggestion of a longer time, a stretch of imagination, the long loneliness and unlikeliness of plain survival.

I do not wish to indulge in whimsy here, something quite the opposite. My father's stories made sense. He was at the throttle of a great machine, a steam locomotive; he made it run, safe and fast and serviceable, a kind of time machine. He was a mover of the universe, not a machine, but a master of machines that served human convenience or need. He did it skillfully, efficently, with pride. He was thus one instrument of a strength that would serve us in good stead, later, when sorrows and absurdities multiplied, and machines unaccountably were concocted to destroy rather than enhance or serve life. I think that fireman fired our imagination. The fires he lit in us are now and again banked, they flare up. He stoked them. As I write this, my brother Philip is jailed in Washington for an act of the imagination. He has dared imagine, and enact (every imaginative act worth talking about is enacted) the death of children, the universal blood letting implicit in the nuclear arms race. I am proud to say that our generation is jailed time and again, for using its imagination, for imagining the hideous technological present, and for implicitly imagining, summoning, another sort of future.

Our father, many years dead, was part of all that. My memories of him are mixed. I do not want to dishonor him by a con job or cosmetics. But his story telling, which to almost any race but the Irish must seem the most errant waste of energy and time, was in fact a kind of transfusion, or bone graft. (I do not know what surgical image will describe the gift, or its outcome. But it was a great thing, that wit, that edge, and a clue worth running after.)

All this brings us time and again to that son, and why he said to us, "when you pray, pray as to a Father. Conjure up the word, the image, the coming and going, the heart and its heartbeat, the way, finally, I come before the one who is always before me. In any case (lest we become too solemn, and forget to play, to smile, neglect our overflow, our holiday) try this: our father . . ."

Let us not be afraid to be ourselves, sorry as that idea may seem. I mean by it that we are not, after all, subject solely to our critics, our censors, our good disliking fellow Christians. We may, after all, be more like our own fathers. And all nicks and cuts aside, what we may remember most vividly are the stories our fathers told us; stories that, as they say these days, *enable*. Simply that, solely that. We may yet forgive the old coot. He enlivened the otherwise dreary scene, he lit it up with his smoky torch, poking into dim recesses, making sense, or at least making nonsense, which, given the world, often come to the same thing.

I think of all this in regard to the Father image of Jesus. On the face of it, of course, there seems to be no one in less need of invoking another, for protector, patron, elder, guru, makeshift or skilled, biological or soulful. Jesus stands firmly on planted feet. He turns serenely to face the direction his voices hint at, whether it be a desert, a mountain, a city to die in. His mind is what a mind should be, by common agreement: single. What do enemies, tempters, spurious voices, pusillanimous vouchers count for, after all? Only in his case, as contrasted with ours, 'after all' is before all. He decided on the direction and gift of his life, before the fact, before the life was wasted or given or calculated. He seems, in the lovely old phrase, to "be beholden" elsewhere.

You, dear reader, might like to reflect at this point whether some person, at some earlier phase of your life, did not tell you a story. And what this story might mean today, as sense-maker, and therefore world maker. The story of a creator — and therefore of our father.

When fathers lose the skill of making stories, everything is changed, and seldom for the better. Shall we think of Father Church in this regard? He has unlearned an earlier skill; today he is therefore querulous and down putting. More law and order, a queasy conformity, make him the blood brother of the latest tin-penny secular savior to come down the pike. Our father cannot tell us where we came from. He has no book of genesis, gorgeous, outrageous, utterly winning, in his stern head. He is confused, not only about our sources, our roots, but about his own. The six days of creation, the apple and the serpent, the murder of brother by brother, the great land trek of the patriarchs, he is silent about these, or he has forgotten the stories. In any case he cannot hold our attention. He loses us.

Certainly the skill was bold and vivid once. We saw it in the skill of Jesus. "There was a man went down from Jerusalem to Jericho, and fell among thieves . . ." "A man had two sons; of whom one said to him one day; Father, give me my share of the inheritance . . ." And then that recurrent theme, the "kingdom of heaven," which was likened to almost everything under the sun, from a pearl to a harvest to a seed to a leaven to a lost coin. But it all comes down in the end, one suspects, to that master image of father and son. The method is quite literally genetic, issuing from a great spirit older than the hills and twice as wise: genesis, exodus, kings, prophets, martyrs, sages. The father whispered this wisdom to the son, the son being (we are told in another image) the word of wisdom itself, who thereupon tells these stories to the tribe, the church, the fathers and sons and mothers and daughters in perpetuum.

We can say "Our Father" only if we are willing to be sons and daughters. The implicatons are far reaching and quite pointed. Let us pray.

Sons and daughters are, because of what they are, also brothers and sisters. The Lord's prayer was given to many, by one. That one rejoices, as Paul tells us, at being "first born of many." You see how the original image, father-son, keeps going, generates itself. Once life gets underway, it cannot easily be contained. That is quite literally the trouble with life: its runaway, expansive, takeover quality. We would like only so much of life as suits our festering egos, our appetites. So death must enter the garden. It was no chance event. Someone made a pact, and left the gate ajar.

But when we follow the gracious invitation to "say it like me," we watch the face of Jesus; we mime him. We would like, in spite of it all, to stand where he stands, to hear the voices he hears, to be trusted with his secrets.

And we are right, in so striving. We need an elder brother. We learn from our peers only to a degree; they are too like us, and we seem at times to share only our delusions. But another has come through all this, and gone beyond.

It is probable that in twenty years or so we will quite literally be unable to imagine what it is like to be human. Few clues, few good stories, no elders, only the machine.

Irish history has it that during the invasions of the early centuries, the monks constructed towers of stone, entered them with the book and the cup, and endured the invasion. The vandals passed through, scorching the earth. The monks descended again to terra firma. The tradition endured.

We too may have to think of ways of preserving our simple literacy, our ability to read the story of our origins, against the machine-tooled onslaught of neo-savagery. Let us pray.

## You Who Are In Heaven

The second phrase, "placing" God (so to speak) "in heaven," may seem to us redundant. Are we thereby to know "where" he is — in some place named, naively, heaven — as well as where he is not (certainly not among us, in the mess and travail, with whose beginning he purportedly had something to do)?

I think not. I think the phrase is crucial to understanding, another hint of the identity of the mysterious one we presume to address. Perhaps any effort of religious understanding is essentially an act of imagination. (I do not suggest such common malpractices as fantasy, vain desire, erotic leanings or the like.) We are to imagine one whose presence is in his absence. So our act of faith is in the presence of his absence.

I am conscious of the irony here, which approaches the absurd, without quite ever veering over that edge.

But perhaps in human dealings also, we incline to make too much of certain kinds of presence — and too little of certain kinds of absence. There is a precious and quite powerful presence which many parents exert on their families. It includes, as a matter of principled tactic, a measure of absence. They say goodbye; they are still here.

Give the sons and daughters space. Give them breathing space. Come, then go. Go, but always return.

And more: certain persons have about them a kind of penumbra, a glow which we properly regard as charismatic. They exert a spiritual force out of all proportion to words, gestures, movement. Their being includes an electric element of stillness, charged with meaning, verve, weight. They are like buddhas, they bring all their life to the concentrated stillness of a moment. We say of them, they are totally here, totally now, emmanuels, godlike, with us.

A freakish culture, on the other hand, abounds in cultural freaks. Ours has produced, among other marvels, parents who are examples only of a kind of smotherhood. At the other extreme are those whose parenthood is a spree of irresponsibility.

The first are omnipresent, alas. The second, utterly absent, spiritually alienated, at odds — also alas.

I take it that the phrase "in heaven" invites us to dwell upon these rhythms of the divine, at once tragic and playful, here ("your will . . . on earth"), and elsewhere — sensitive, brooding, responsive; and then olympian, far from us as hell from heaven.

But Jesus told a story about this phrase, "in heaven." As one might expect from his nuanced imagination, the story plays the multiple rhythms, notes, keys.

The story is a heart stopper. A special poignancy: the son tells us of his father (and ours). Something of presence and absence. A genesis story to start with, about a land owner who fosters, humanizes, applies skill and care to his holdings. There is a business air to it. The owner is, as we say, "involved." This astute owner-farmer, having seen to all necessary chores and tasks, planting, wall building, installation of a wine press, raising of a watch tower, renting out the property — a veritable six days of creation — then he withdraws, retires from the scene, more exactly "goes abroad." (And on the seventh day, he rested from his labors; or, "our father who are in heaven.")

It need not be stressed that the meticulous care of fostering the vineyard, the property, the world, saves the "going abroad," the being "in heaven," from reclusiveness, olympian deatchment. The one who goes abroad will return. There is to be an accounting. Justice demands it, austerely, insistently.

32

For contracts have been let. A network of justice, accountability, was laid down by mutual agreement. There is benefit to both sides; there are burdens, labors, sharing assumed by both sides.

The owner has not yet revealed himself, in toto. Judgement is the theme, as the story develops. Or, if that is too strong a word, an accounting, in justice. We might conclude at this stage that the point of the story is a simple business arrangement, to be consummated on both sides, with good will and integrity. Alas.

The harvest time approaches. It was of course envisioned from the beginning that a division of profits would be made, as there had been a division of labor, a mutual investment. So far, so good. Servants are sent, equals of the laborers and tenants, to see to such matters.

And at this point, the scene turns nightmarish, begins to exceed all normal conduct. "They took his servants, thrashed one, killed another, and stoned a third."

Were there other issues at stake, other grievances unspoken? We are not told. The story simply collides with our expectation. Suddenly we are transported to a realm of the irrational, the demented. The tenants not only refuse just payment, they humiliate, punish, murder.

And if the treatment of his servants is not bad enough, the reaction of the landowner is also, in quite another direction, excessive, grotesque. He resolves, apparently, to outdo the enemy; not in revenge, but in forgiveness. (Is this what it means to "be in heaven"?) He swallows hard, buries the past. (We had best keep our eyes on this seigneur; he is a very demon of unpredictable, surreal conduct, out of this world.)

Scene two proceeds as though scene one had not run its bloody course. He sends other servants to collect the rent, the harvest dues. He acts as though servants were literally infinite in number, endlessly available. This is the fiction, a fiction of forgiveness which, in the present case, is pure fact, serious truth. "He sent more servants, this time a larger number; and they did the same to them."

In the light of history, the "servants" of the story can be none other than the prophets, who indeed die gratuitously. And the story is cool about their death, because it is not, after all, the land owner who murders them. He only sends them on a just errand. The crime indeed is elsewhere. The facts of history are in. Like every good parable, the moral of this one broods offstage. No one pushes it forward.

One might even cry out: the true criminal is the landowner. His crime is his forgiveness, irresponsible, irrespective. The author of history seems totally ignorant of history. How can he do these things? He acts as though humans were not evil at all, as though our evil had never stained his face with tears, tightened his heart with dread. How can such innocence not be criminal?

He tries a third time. (Is this what it means to dwell "in heaven"? — that one tries, over and over again, against the evidence, against the tide?) "I will send my son." Is the son more dear than the servants? Is it reasonable to risk the life of the son, when the servants have been violated, abused, murdered?

The parable, like every good parable, raises more questions than it answers. In any case, we have a kind of last ditch effort at forgiveness. "I will send my son . . . they will respect my son."

This is what a father does, who dwells "in heaven." He hopes against hope. He sends his son, when all else has failed. That is to say, the best wine is kept for the last. The first and second attempts, which were such bloody failures, are wiped out; no record. "I will send my son."

And the result is predictable, any other outcome absurdly unthinkable. Could it not be alleged against this owner that he actually provokes the worst, in invoking the best? He should have known better, should have studied a primer entitled *Criminal Tendencies in Human Nature; A Psycho-Historical Study of Innate Evil, Including Also a Learned Discourse on Original Sin and Public Consequences?*

He is incurably naive. (Is this what it means to dwell "in

heaven"?) He sent his own son, all else failing. Was this in consequence of his dwelling "in heaven" a properly celestial decision, one so far beyond our capacities, our understanding, our reaction to evil as to take our true measure, the measure of our possibility — a measure our despair has never allowed us?

In any case, dwelling "in heaven" is no obstacle to the most sublime commerce with earth. "I will send my son."

God is God, the earthbound are also themselves.

To be God means this: when all else fails, you send your son.

To be earthbound means this: when murder has failed, you murder again.

Thus the perfect obstinacy of forgiveness is opposed by the baleful obstinacy of death. Who then can win?

Evil, in the sense that death brings life down, servants, more servants, prophets, more prophets, then the son. Against death there is no recourse.

Still it is never recorded that the father, in story or fact, reneged on his first design: go, be present, tell the truth, demand an accounting. And if required, die.

It was required, invariably, human nature being — as the cynics say — human nature. (And God, be it added, being God.)

Still, life prevails. ("Win" is, after all, an odious word here.) An act of God prevails, that act which began with the absurd mission, and which death could but interrupt, not abort. "He raised up his son Jesus."

But death was the first act. They entered into conspiracy to kill the son, to seize his inheritance. It was no sudden spasm of violence, his murder. The story is icy as a court record. "This is the heir; come, let us kill him and get his inheritance."

Is this what it means to dwell "in heaven," that in foresight of consequences, one continues to pursue a spiral of mercy? Always more: first the prophets, then more prophets, generations of prophets. Then finally, in a last outburst of anguished compassion, send "my Son!"

This heavenly being is capable of most unwordly conduct. He cannot calculate gains and losses. (There are in fact no gains to calculate. The story is the very opposite of cynical, but it is surgically, cruelly exact, this tale of murder that lurks in the vineyard and is its truest fruit, the dark and merciless things that are behind possessions.

Possessions? Say rather, we are possessed, by his spirit, or by demons. For this reason there is no hint of moral neutrality in the vineyard. The tenants do not say to one another, come let us bargain with the servants, with the son. They are reasonable beings, they understand cupidity. "After all, we are not profitless servants, we have turned a dollar or two beyond expectation. Sensible people cannot but appreciate this . . . " Nothing of this. They are in possession of the vineyard, they have nine points of the law on their side. They are also possessed by the vineyard, the demon in possession is named death. He strikes no bargains.

At this point the heavenly being collides with the earthly beings. "They seized him, flung him out of the vineyard, and slew him." They indulged in no pretext, explanation, dialogue, indictment, or defense. They were jury, judge, executioners in one. It is the passion of Jesus, stripped of its mad charade of legitimacy. Herod, Pilate, the mob, the sanhedrin — "they seized him, flung him out of the vineyard, and slew him."

This is what it means to be the prophet, son, emissary, of the one who dwells "in heaven."

We should not miss an added irony. The story is told by the son, the final emissary. It is autobiographical — not, in the ordinary sense of the word, an account of one's life up to this or that moment. No, this story dares penetrate the future, penetrates hearts like a rapier, twists the weapon there. It says, I come among you bearing the truth. And you will murder me; it is simple as that.

This is an impolitic way of commending one's cause. It might even be called provocative, saying, in effect, do your worst; until then, you will never repent. Do your worst, which has already been done in your hearts. Your lust for property, money, is already murderous, idolatrous. All that remains is to enact it.

Is this what it means to be son of the one who dwells in heaven? One has such acute knowledge of the human heart, such love for humans, that one dares, provokes, calls forth the demons, into the light of day; to be named, to do their worst? That one offers one's life as surety, as field for that combat? A socratic exchange closed the episode. "What do you think the outcome of all this will be when the land owner returns? He will make a bad end of these murderers, he will hand over the vineyard to others, who will give him his just share of things, at harvest time."

The One who dwells in heaven is author of three great actions on earth. He rents out the vineyard, sends his son, and he returns. We have, in one parable, the classical biblical themes of creation, redemption, and judgement.

It is the very opposite of detached deity, of this or that myth. Fiercely, passionately, madly in love. Lover, spouse, friend. Hosea the prophet was right. So are the mystics.

We do well to keep our eyes on the one who was sent, if we would gain a clue to the style, method, grace of the one who sends. We have seen that dwelling "in heaven" does not imply a two-world platonic theory, but a constant transaction of life and love.

A human father, the father of any of us, may be thought in faith to dwell "in heaven" after death. Insofar as he now is believed to share, in an intimate and immediate way, the life of God, the outlook of God, the moral and ethical mind of God, especially in regard to right conduct among humans.

Such a faith often transfigures memory. One thinks of one's father after death (perhaps after a long lapse of time) as someone of wisdom, whose aphorisms are worth committing to memory and living by, whose life, as life goes forward, makes good sense. Faults and frictions tend to fall in place, or fade utterly from memory.

Is it somewhat thus with Jesus, who was found "obedient unto death"? In any case, we must not invoke that transfiguration of memory too easily, cheaply. The reward of obedience toward the one who dwells "in heaven" is one's own rebirth, resurrection. But the cost of such obedience is a dolorous one: death on the cross. Let us not take lightly the attitude of Jesus to such a father and his will. We know little about the psychology of a divine one (perhaps not much more about the psychology of human beings). And at times it seems that our knowledge of either is almost entirely corrupted by our American journey to the void.

Still, we do know that he sweat blood, and that this spartan man, whose stern exactions he first tested out in his own frame, cried aloud in the garden and on the cross — the most terrible cry in creation, the cry of a heroic being who has touched the depths.

Thus the price of creatureliness, or of obedience, of which one modern mystic has said simply that it is a "need of the soul."

Jesus seems to have been heavily conscious of death, as the story implies. It is only in John's gospel that his death is relieved of its tragic foreshadow, and attains the distance and light of an epiphany.

Still, a holy one would be of little help or meaning to us, if his story ended with himself still living. We make cruel demands on our founding fathers — or mothers. The price is their death. And they must of course die well, as they must live transcendently. This is what the earthbound demand insatiably: holiness.

In the parable, this earthly holy one, the son of the owner, comes toward his fate as though accoutered in a Greek mask, impassively. He comes because he is sent, that is all. He is the simple unwavering instrument of another's will. It is as though his life has no significant moments, no choices, until the moment of death; but then his death precipitates a judgement, long delayed against the killers.

The story, brief and stark as it is, means only to invite us further, into the transformation of Jesus; from the one who lives and dies well, into the one who also, with his father, dwells "in heaven," himself becomes a heavenly creature.

It was his destiny, it is our own. I believe.

Still, a nagging question arises. Can we know today, in America, what it is to die well?

We know a great deal about murder. In the urban back-yards, in the world at large. We are like a Mafia to the world, on twenty-four hour call, under contract to all the colonels, first secretaries, shahs, kings, juntas, entrepreneurs, oil sheiks, banana dictators. We will go anywhere, any time, to kill. For a price. For a slogan. For energy, for markets. And at times, as in ten or fifteen years of war in Vietnam, for the hell of it.

A mega-industry of death thus arises, a development peculiar to our culture and time. It is against such a blood-ridden culture, the very atmosphere and climate we breathe, work in, make decisions in, that our faith raises the question of a good life and virtuous death.

The incompatibility of America with the gospel is a moral chasm which time and folly only serve to widen. It grows harder even to take such soundings of the chasm as are necessary for sanity itself. Our instruments are awry. The church cannot help measure the chasm, or sound warnings concerning the worsening earth fault. She is forever, fussily, absurdly, hopelessly, trying to bridge the chasm, to walk across it in thin air, to declare a miracle when good sense and courage suffice to see what eyes cannot help seeing.

The Bomb should be enough to indicate where we are going. If, say, the neutron bomb had suddenly been announced, without more than thirty intervening years of nuclear digging and filling, it would be relatively easy today to raise or invoke an outcry. Perhaps. But the initial shock was the only shock. The rest has been sweet talk in a moral nursery, perched on the edge of a volcano, cooing infantilism, keepers and kept.

The initial explosion of Hiroshima was, after all, set off in the heat and frenzy of a war, and was therefore self-justified: and it justified every infamy that followed in the nuclear chain. The first step was everything, as the saying goes. It encompassed the whole journey — into the void.

Thus the processing and packaging of cheap death, of death for a price, of the death of the unwanted, of unwanted nations or minorities or children or the unborn or the abstract distant Muscovites or Pekinese — all this is accompanied by a spiritual regression of momentous import. We can no longer die well, we can only kill well. This may well be the judgement of the future on the American adventure: they killed with a bang, they died with a whimper.

Now at a first glance (which is the inevitable cultural glance, and the acculturated religious glance as well) it must be admitted that Jesus seems to have died badly. He seems to have been unresigned: he was certainly not granted a peaceable last hour in his own bed. He perished, in fact, out of cycle, whether of age or descendants. His friends were so acutely scandalized as to be unable to bear his bloody presence, and by and large fled the scene.

Who wants enemies surrounding his death? To push matters further, enemies who have prevailed, whose lies and hatreds have fingered one, have created a legal cloud of plausibility? The death is normalized, it is according to law. History, decency, religion, all are upheld, and applaud the act.

Moreover, the cataclysm seems to have thoroughly demoralized the victim.

He cries out for relief, no relief is forthcoming. Something called "providence," "the Father," is appealed to, and revealed publicly as a sham or delusion. It is a scene of utter disarray, on earth; and, if you will, in heaven.

Who could possibly recommend such a death to those seeking meaning, or faith, or relief from America?

And yet relief from America (or Babylon, or Rome, or Assyria), or Russia, or China, is exactly what this death offers. Just as it offers an example, and reverses the methods of the abovementioned powers and principalities.

The way heroes die appalls and frightens and repels. Such deaths make us ill. They bring close to us, not only the barbarities of public power; they dramatize the demons and angels that struggle within us. They tell us we are mortal, and cowardly and faithless. They tell us the truth.

They raise again a question which we (and our culture) had thought once and for all, decently and sweetly interred: How does one die well, in a bad time for humans (which we are constantly being told is a good time — but as we suspect, only for inhumans)? As death by violence multiplies, the non-violent death of the Lord, the death of the one who suffers violence rather than inflicting it, offers a great hope.

And as death becomes the common method of securing military advantage, markets, inheritances, oil fields, gold, uranium, nuclear secrets, and the like, the death of the one who desires nothing, covets nothing, clings to nothing — this death offers a great hope.

And as heroic souls are continually being tested in the fires of torture, prison, kangaroo courts and the like, the example of the one who endured and won through, also offers a great hope.

But we are still speaking of human matters, in a restricted scope. It is God who suffers and dies on our wood. By this act, heaven is opened, in the old classic phrase of our childhood. Which is to say, the human has entered the realm of the divine; the human has been reborn to its proper glory. We are admitted to a new existence, we have become a "new creation."

I am among the first to say that I find such expressions both exhilarating and perplexing. Their literal meaning, it seems to me, needs to be pondered over a lifetime of varied, joyous, damnably difficult and soul testing experience, before we can hope to extract an inkling of their meaning for ourselves — that is to say a meaning that is energizing, loving, hopeful and non-contentious. The short cut, deviously hewn out by many young conversion experts who infest our airports, bus terminals and main streets today, does not seem to answer the need I speak of. With hardly any experience of the lives they accost, and hardly any equipment that might be termed evangelical (but with a great measure of self will and malice) these fundamentalist hell raisers attempt to drive home the love of God under hammer blows of contention. Invariably this service is rendered for an exacted price. I am not sure I can be pulled and pushed into rebirth in this way. Not that I want to be, a sacred enlistment being no more attractive to my rambunctious soul than a military one.

On such occasions, fleeing a plague I cannot combat, I reflect ruefully that not only governments are skilled in fascist ploys. Churches living under such governments seem hell bent on the same lock-stepping progress toward the same absurd, lethal goal. O God, leave us to our gods, is their cry.

In a bad time, let us comfort our soul with the example, the living presence of Jesus martyr, and the presence of the vast "cloud witnesses" who, in his image, attained the human apothesis through the ages down to Stephen Biko, in our own day — the presence of those who die well, that we may not perish in the second death.


It would be interesting to reflect on the word "heaven" as an index of human expectation. Nirvana, surcease, relief, reward, eternal sleep, pleasure dome, world apart, kingdom of the spirit, after life, Eden, paradise — most of the common expressions wear a kind of lunar look out there somewhere in the great beyond . . . We are like those who have imbibed only the syndicated syrup of mortician advertisements. In the presence of death, the tactic is to keep the living so narcoticized by the hyped beauty of a corpse that they are unconcious of having their pockets fleeced. The same images are appropriated bodily by popular religion. What it first stole from us was the bible.

Still such a larceny can be repaired. And it ought not be accounted an act of virtue to allow the crime to go on indefinitely. The fact that a momentous biblical reality has been mistranslated, misappropriated, lawlessly demolished, ought not restrain us from searching out and restoring it once more.

We have seen from one parable that the biblical meaning of dwelling "in heaven", encompasses the process of creation (the land owner goes away), incarnation and mission ("I will send my son"), and finally judgement (he will wreak havoc on those evil doers).

It is all action, transaction, passion, tragedy, history. In the end, it is love that governs, impels, unites, reconciles, binds up. Indeed, we imply a great deal when we invoke the heavenly one.

## Hallowed Be Your Name

It is probably useful to watch Jesus at prayer, before we try to set up our own prayer house. To watch him, at least in this sense, that we want to absorb something of his world view, his father view, human view, ethic, sense of God and himself. How did he verify this petition?

We might push the question further. Why did he pray at all, a prayer of petition? (The whole Lord's prayer is one long sigh of longing for that which is not yet, one long sigh of hope for what may yet be . . . ) He petitions the Father for some "good" to be given — which good, it must be understood, is already "given"! Indeed, to be the Father is to have the name Father infinitely blessed, hallowed. So then what?

Without becoming pedantic, one could reflect that the first hallowing, blessing, bestowed on a Father, is to be Father of such a son — Jesus. It is in him that the "hallowing" petition is first of all granted; and then some. This is a truth we may take with perfect seriousness, since it was an element of the luminous self understanding of Jesus.

Again we do well to avoid as far as possible the stain of the platonic. It might be profitable to think of Father-Son forever fervently locked in an embrace of understanding and love in some seventh heaven. The genesis of the son, we are told by reliable theologians, is from eternity. But this is hardly to our point. And from the point of view of the bible, it either precedes the first page, or follows mysteriously on the last one — which is to say, the eternal generation of the son by the Father

45

is no part of our history, nor of this world. While we might wish to emulate the "perfect detachment" of the mystics (who are in fact neither perfect nor detached) and dwell on the eternal aspect of the divine, it would seem that Jesus invites us in another direction. Else why a prayer that presumably fell from human lips, on a certain day, in a given corner of our world? A prayer that moreover, is incurably worldly, concrete, dwelling in time and place? The hallowing of the name of God has therefore this aspect: a working out, an experience, a passion, a knot-hole of diminution and death, a rebirth to be undergone.

We hear Jesus instructing us in this prayer, and we know nothing fraudulent falls on our ears, but a plea for right order, an ethic of love, a world that is no stranger to the voice of God. We have moreover the cold comfort of a larger history. We know what the plea cost the son who uttered it.

Without indulging in despair, or in a kind of idolatry of Jesus which leaves us free and easy of moral responsibility, we might think of the crossroads at which the son stood, in uttering such a plea and instructing us in its uses.

The world, then or now, is not greatly disposed to honor the name of God. I confess that in writing this sentence, I am indulging in an understatement that would make the angels rush to judgement. Indeed, the dishonor of God seems at times to be the passionate vocation of worldly powers and structures — then and now; at the time of the prayer's first utterance, and today when we flounder about, trying not to utter the prayer with an utterly devious heart.

If on the other hand, we summon up the moral atmosphere of a bucolic Saint Francis among the daisies (a saint who of course never existed outside the craven minds of post-childhood children) in which ideal and unstained place the Lord said, "Blessed be your name," then we miss the point entirely. The prayer falls apart in our mouth, like mold. It has the stench of death about it, or of romantic paganism, which is roughly the same thing.

Most of all we miss the charged irony that underlies the

Lord's very existence, and his words. The mildest seeming utterances, the most liturgically correct, the phrases which seem entirely directed "on high"; in reality, if we understand, they tighten the spring of crisis, they heighten the conflict between worldly powers and the 'method' of God. Indeed, words like "mild," "liturgical," "on high," are altogether our invention, not his.

His crime was a long time gathering its true and indictable character. It gathered, it came to a head. Certainly an element of the crime was such words as these, uttered in a political and religious scene that was both politically tense and ethically corrupt. The words bear the weight of that world, which was leaning like a crazy tower, just before falling. When it fell, it crushed him utterly.

Still, in the old crude phrase, he had asked for it. Not because he prayed this way, or indeed some other way. Words after all are cheap and errant, they go where the wind goes. (Though perhaps we might grant that in his world, words were considerably less debased than in ours.) No, his crime was his style, his stance in the world, his moral maladjustment, his intemperate commentary on the comic-tragic game. He would not be an inoffensive god, nor a servile one, in the image of idols men and women passionately desired — to worship, to prosper under, to pay tribute to, to sacrifice blood to, to die for.

None of this. His prayer pointed straight to the Father. No strange gods.

And that of course was unacceptable. It meant he was an iconoclast, more precisely, a breaker of idols.

As Jesus viewed it, religion was, in the nature of things, a matter of conflict and crisis. Bloodletting. Death. His own.

We see things otherwise. Our hearts are divided as the broken fork of a dry stick, we like to prate about "pure religion," "pure worship," and so on. We could make our peace with this Jesus, if only he would retire to some mountainside or desert (which indeed he did on occasion) and there fulfill our longing for *nada,* for nothingness, for the void, for the comfort of pure ascent, pure withdrawal. No world, only heaven. No intrusive human names (those names of need, of illness, of despair, of brokenness — our names, the names of those we love), no, only the name of God: our god, certainly; his god, uncertainly.

The above is by no means intended to defame the mystics who dwell apart on the world's mountain fastnesses or deserts. Thank God for them, the true God. But to speak of Jesus, it seems clear that when he went to the desert to pray, it was to be tried to his soul's marrow by demons, tempting him with regard to a worldly or godlike vocation in this world; and when he went to the mountain to pray, it was to receive some light, in the sight of his chosen disciples. That thread, that linkage, that umbilical joining him to our world and time, was never broken. How we would like to break it, once and for all! He never broke it. In this we might sense a difference between him and ourselves.

There was a father who had two sons. One he named High Jinks; the other Holier Than Thou.

The naming was not done lightly; this father did nothing lightly. He was rich and noble, and in this world, the combination spelled trouble and sorrow, the bowing of an old head, a fortune that was a misfortune. But then he took thought (thought was all that was required) and he said; I will settle my riches and my troubles on two sons, whom I will beget from my forehead, and whom I will name as named above. The first will be called High Jinks because Jinks means fun and high jinks means outrageous fun. Alas, I have never had any fun, high or low, in all my life. And the second I will name Holier Than Thou. He will be holier than me. Because if I were holier than I am, I would be free of all this real estate, this unreal estate, these bank deposits, these spitting camels and muttering tribes. But my second son will be free of all that. Don't ask me how, since I will settle on his unsuspecting infant pate the half of my kingdom, half of everything from sunup to sundown. The other half I will settle on High

Jinks, but I have no very great hopes of him. Even before the fact, I am willing to resign myself to the depreciation of everything he touches. Half a loaf is better than none. I will sacrifice half my kingdom to secure the other half, in Holier Than Thou. Holier, that is, than me.

That one will be my boyo. (The king actually smiled to himself under his night cap as he settled to sleep.) That one will be my tireless runner, Holier Than Thou, my obedient one, my well rewarded errand boy. Fleet he will be, bringing cheer to the heart, the comfort of this rickety old age of mine. And the king turned his nose aside, under the covers, for it was very cold, and slept.

That night he dreamed of High Jinks and Holier Than Thou. He dreamed they stepped out of his forehead, which opened like a stone archway and tumbled them out, and closed again. In his dream they were two red infants, then they walked about, then they lisped imperfectly, and finally when he awoke in the morning, there stood at his bedside two handsome strapping youths. One was black of poll, with eyes of midnight. The other was a blond wonder with a face like dawn. The first had mischief in his eyes and self will, a cat's gleam; the other was all listener, intent and wary. High Jinks held in hand a covered plate that bore three hot buttered croissants. Holier Than Thou was stirring a bowl of steaming chocolate. The king sat up, opened one eye and said to himself: well, quite a beginning, indeed. Welcome, boys. Sit down.

He passed the day getting to know his sons. The three talked together, the king listened, the sons were all vivacity and enthusiasm. They tramped through the barns and toured the fields, met the farm workers and the house keepers. Everyone agreed that Holier Than Thou resembled his father, was serious and devout, an altogether good son. Now the old man can die content; he's got someone go carry on, the upstairs maid said to the butler (and was reproved for it, which didn't a whit change her mind). Even the starchy old chauffeur agreed with a portentous nod that Holier Than Thou looked like the infallible comfort of his father's decline. The chauffeur nodded and then nodded again, just to cap an opinion that was now a dogma.

About High Jinks there were second and third thoughts. Who was this kid anyway? By noon the boys were an overgrown 18 years old. But whereas Holier had all the gravity of position and place, Jinks was bold and racy and beyond predicting. He wouldn't hang around. He kept wandering off, humming to himself, snooping around corners and behind closed doors. Life on the plantation seemed more of a lark than a task. And that face — where did he come from, anyway? He resembled nobody anybody could think of, neither his father, who managed to be both plump and rawboned, an old farmer gone to seed, nor the family portraits in the hallways, going back in fairly unbroken line to the start of things (a rather fish-faced sepia ancestor about whom nobody knew much). But this kid! In mid-afternoon, now about 19 years of tomfoolery under one hat, Jinks loped into the barn, saddled one of the best horses, and took off across the hills, humming to himself some ribald snatch he'd picked up from the grooms. Oh, he was a quick learner in some directions!

He hung around the place when he wanted to, he was off to town when the itch took him, he had his own sweet way and his own sweet will. He was bounden to none, he came and went, free-loaded where he could, cajoled when he must.

So far my story. Its only virtue is that it corresponds to a story Jesus told. Which roughly speaking, goes like this. A man had two sons. He went and said to one, my son, go and work in the vineyard today. But High Jinks tossed his brush of hair and sassed back: Not on your life, daddy. I've got a luscious party waiting for me at the cross roads just down the pike. Man, is she a dish! We're going to town together, daddy-o in your buckboard (he dug his finger, not so playfully, in the old man's Adam rib, which was missing, and therefore a sorespot, as can be imagined). Now you go find that Holy Roller brother of mine and you tell him to get off his holy ass and harness up that nag and jump into those vineyards feet first. Come January me and my chick are going to need some of that bottled bubble. I ain't promised nothing, you unnerstand, but it's just possible there may be weddin' bells in our future. And he turned on his boot with a grin and went off humming an Elvis number.

His father went sorrowfully to look for Holier Than Thou. He found him in his attic room, boning up on the book of Deuteronomy for a charismatic meeting he was to lead that night. Holier was very hip on chapters 3 to 14, the law and order parts where God was nailing down certain crimes and punishments in great detail. Holier could almost hear the hammers whanging away. He was not pleased when the old man came in.

He looked up, keeping his finger on verse 78 of chapter 19, busy and angry as a wasp in a dry bottle. Finger on the saving text, you could see "I'm HTT, don't hassle me," written all over him.

The father started to explain. The grapes were ripe, the weather right, delay would risk the whole summer's work. Holier listened; he didn't look too holy. He made a kind of slow and obvious to-do, closing the bible, collecting his notes, putting his holiness to one side with a kind of subdued tantrum. What a bunghole of a life, an old doddering daddo, a Rhet Butler of a brother whoring and drinking and playing fast and loose with the family name. He thought such thoughts; he kept them to himself.

His eyes were on high, as though he were agreeing to have his head chopped off for the one true faith. But he didn't look so holy. He looked like he'd like nothing better than to spray his father with holy spit. Finally he said yes, he'd go (Damnit). The father went away mumbling something about sorry, and how I thank you son, you always come through. All of which was received with a look blacker than midnight behind closed shutters, if you can imagine such a look out of the bluest of blue eyes.

Meantime back at the cross roads, cruising along in his pa's buckboard, High Jinks had taken thought.

51

Poor old bones, he said to himself, I've half a mind to turn around and go do that grape picking after all. What the hell. 'Spose I do stand Chickie up, who by now is undoubtedly biting her lil ol nails to the bone, waiting for lover boy. I said I wouldn't pick 'em, I'll go do it. So long, baby, I'll peel a grape in your memory . . . He turned the horse's head around with a mighty jerk, loped back to the grape arbors, humming that old Elvis tune. And worked there all day, to sundown and past, a grinning grape-picking Bacchus of a boy.

And meantime. We left Holier looking like a captive thunder-er cloud in the attic. Trouble was, he was obliged by his religion to put a good face on a bad scene. So he slammed the bible shut and went out of the house and across the yard, looking as though holy butter wouldn't melt in his mouth, all the while feeling like a butter churn full of brimstone. Muttering away. (The servants could take his buzzing for holy prayer). Damn old man, irreligious old fart, comes in with his work orders, there goes my holy day, there goes God out the window. How can a body live a Christian life in this place? And he kicked the dog and spat at the cat, being by now out of earshot and sight of the holy trackers and admiring looks.

He was hitching up the horse when the light dawned. He'd said he'd go, but who said he had to? He could change his mind, couldn't he? He was free, white and 21, wasn't he? That fool brother did as he damned pleased, didn't he? He tossed the harness down in a heap of horse shit, shut the barn door with a bang. When last seen, he was hotfooting it over the hills and far away. . .

Well, to go on in Jesus' words: The father said to the first son, go and work in the vineyards today. He answered, I will not go, but afterward thought better of it and went. The man then went and said the same thing to the second who answered, certainly sir; and then did not go. Which of the two honored the father? The first, they said.

Hallowed be thy name.

The story is half playful and totally serious. Playful; conscious of quirks and knots of the soul. Who has not said a resounding NO — to life, to another, to a distateful unavoidable job, to a bad day, to an unpleasant child, to his own soul — and then promptly or jocosely or morosely or with half a heart or with a full heart, reversed gears, turned around? And who has not said yes too hastily, too thoughtlessly, with no attention to the cost, the weight too heavy, the sacrifice too long — and reversed that, and come out with an ungracious self-denying, truth-obscuring utterly unpredictable NO: a No that for all its wrong, is still closer to the truth of our dark moods and selfishness and smallness of heart. And to that degree it is perhaps more acceptable than the devious smile of the mask that so well concealed the churning mad doubleness of our soul.

Who truly hallowed the name of the father? The son who said no and changed it to yes; the son who said yes, and then refused? The hearers answered, the first son. They said it, you see, in spite of themselves. They were much more on the other side; the skill they were constantly dusting off and improving was the skill at saying yes, when they really meant no; the camouflaged refusal, the great refutation; of God, of life, of community. And these were religious people. They were holy people. It might even define them to say their lives said yes when they really meant no.

— They said *yes* at their worship and *no* with their good solid paganism.

— They said *yes* to the closed bible and *no* to the first and greatest command.

— They sang a resounding *yes* when the hymns were struck up, and just as resounding (and a good deal colder) *no,* when the poor appeared at the door.

— All sorts of meaningless *yeses;* and all sorts of substantial *nos.* The *yes* was a shrug, a lip service, the *no* was where they put their money.

That was why, for instance, their church lay in a morass of cultural mire, without a sigh or a protest. And that was why the government rode high and mighty over the powerless. The former because the Church had become a consummate chorus, a crowd of crowd pleasers; yesyesyes. And the government could count on emasculated religion to front for its own gods, with taxes, with White House Sunday magic shows. And when war was the bloody policy (which is to say, almost always) it could count on the Church for the consummate conspiracy, which is to say, the crime of silence.

There was really no conceivable crisis which could bring heavy friction between these two millstones. They ground away, yes, no and maybe; twin powers they were in fact; one coming down heavy as gravity on stone, the other stolidly upholding law and order. But each, from a Christian point of view, had an uncanny (and from a biblical point of view, passing strange) vocation: it was that of creating martyrs. Grinding bones to make imperial bread . . . .

Jesus, we are assured, hallowed the name of the Father. The prayer he commends to us arose from his deep heart's core. He was of that race of rare individuals who do not beckon where they have not led, or place on others' shoulders burdens they have not carried many a mile themselves, including a yes that means what it says.

We are entitled also to conclude that the parable of the quixotic sons tells us something of Jesus himself. (Was ever a good story told, one genuinely lit up with the truth of things, that did not at the same time tell something about the story teller? I think not.)

One does not want to overdo things; we are not "in on" the mystery of Jesus. We are far from the saints and mystics. Still, Paul tells us Jesus "learned obedience by things he suffered." The phrase is strongly suggestive of one who, like the rest of us, had in large measure to improvise life, who learned as he went, who trusted where he could not see clearly, who was beckoned in directions which remained maddeningly obscure (or in one instance maddeningly clear: the instance being that of his own death).

We are walking a tight-rope here. But every sane task has something of dizziness, of height and the unknown about it.

And it seems as though the mystery of Jesus bears some likeness to the mystery of self-understanding. We live, like a spider, along the line; we walk that line of life, at our peril. But the reward is this: if we are truly living, and at least now and then laying something out, risking an inch or so of our sweet skin, we gain insight into the life of Jesus as well. We too must learn obedience (creatureliness, a rightful place in an organic universe) by the thing which we suffer. Or we refuse to suffer, and therefore remain ignorant as stones in a garden of living beings.

One way of putting that process, that learning, is the way the story puts it: to come out of a moral dilemma, a command that balks our way, galls and hurts — to come out of such a time, with a *yes* to God on our lips. But a *yes* that has barely won through, in a very thicket of reasons (enticing, plausible, menacing, persuasive) for saying no.

There is a sense in which the parable of the two sons is the parable of only one son. The parable is speaking of the doubleness in our wills, a doubleness that can so easily become a moral duplicity. It speaks of the "two roads" that "diverged in a wood," of the *yes* that is half-hearted, and is swung around like an errant vane by the next wind that blows no — and again, the initial, hasty, self-willed *no* that is repented, and recovered from.

Not many of us have sweated out this double intent, unto a sweat of blood, a matter of literal life and death — our life, our death. Nor will the majority of us, presumably, die by public execution. The world within us cushions our souls against the titanic virulence of the world out there. Still, since we are resolved not to be heroic, and are not, on the other hand, irremediably evil, we taste, now and then, the bitter doubleness of the single son. Our hope is that perhaps we can still call ourselves sons and daughters, that we claim some spiritual kinship, that we have not entirely given up. Nor, by a long shot, are we given up on. So we go on, because we hope on.

St. Thomas Aquinas, who speculated that Jesus had no great cause to exercise the virtue of hope (since in some unique sense, he "saw" God) nevertheless says that Jesus did hope. He hoped for us. A lovely and strengthening thought.

It is in dying that we are invited to cast off the last of those *nos* that, like a sea choked with sharks, bring us the wrong death. We are not to be shark bait, eaten alive; we are to go out gently, on a tide of love. It is in his death that Jesus attains the stature and clarity and focus of the unique son. The doubleness disappears, the dying cry is one of victory, exultation. The holy name is hallowed, honored, glory is the son's earning.

Hallowed be thy name. May we die well.

## Your Kingdom Come

The prayer addresses not a king, but a father. So the prayer goes, in its proper setting, Our father . . . thy kingdom come; not, Our King . . . thy kingdom come.

An interesting development of the old testament metaphor, which, whatever its shortcomings, was at least consistent: Kingdom, king.

Why the transition? Consistency can itself become a dogma. Metaphors harden, in time, into literal concrete. Jesus does not only inherit images; he plays with them, the sign of a living mind, as contrasted with an inert one.

He does not even hesitate at times to commit that bugbear fault the purists wince at. He actually mixes his metaphors! as in the present one.

We are perhaps to be surprised, jolted; a light is struck in an unexpected place. What does he mean, anyway, by the Father's kingdom? What would it look like? And what is he implicitly rejecting in the old metaphor?

When a king becomes a parent, remaining all the while a king, then for at least one person, his daughter or son, something new has been added. Not added, conjoined. There is a child in the house, a person, a near peer: first a dependant, a learner and listener; then an inheritor, an equal.

Now taking the biology as metaphor, we have a king and a kingdom; but with a difference. A whole realm of sons and daughters. All are called, are reborn; all inherit, all struggle to emerge as equal voices, persons stepping into their own destiny, shaping their response to the world and time and money and power and responsibility. We have a kingdom which is quite simply a community of daughters and sons. And the community will prosper — not insofar as the king is high on his throne, high on his power, but insofar as the community takes up, in every case, the burden and glory of humankind, the risks and conflicts that are inevitable when lives are heard from, when sons and daughters come into their own.

The kingdom's coming, the coming of such a community, is a metaphor of time itself. It is not the time of moral neutrals and the unconcerned, who have no better symbols of their captivation by this world than the instruments of time they consult. It is a time of conscience, in view of a promise.

This is abstractly put, and the genius of Jesus is not in abstractions. It is rather his precise skill, ranging over the human scene, of portraying life and death, his religious patrimony, telling of the simple evidence of his eyes. All this. And breathing life into "eyes that see not, ears that hear not."

We have said that he plays with figures, images. I mean that he is not a slave, not lodged in a rut, not a mimic of true greatness. He sees afresh, he makes it new. It is remarkable that in the 13th chapter of St. Matthew, where Jesus offers images of the kingdom of the father in progress, there is scarcely an echo of the old testament. There are two direct citations, one from the psalms and one from Isaiah. But for the rest, he strikes out from his own.

One speculates as to why. The father image seized on the kingly one and absorbed it; a generative image in place of one that had grown stereotyped, inert, even ominous.

How? If God were king in the image of an earthly satrap, pharaoh, colonel, shah, general — then what was to be said of the subjects? How imply their rebirth, joy, adulthood, freedom? How imply the conflicts and heady and icy weathers of love, the struggle toward mutual respect and shared resolve? Whether we look at our time or his, or at the history he was drawing on, we are not reassured. Indeed, the vicious realities of human kingship won no great enthusiasm from

Israel's God. Quite the opposite.

No wonder Jesus started over.

"Such crowds gathered round him that he got into a boat and sat there. The people all stood on the beach, and he told them many things in parables."

The "many things" were indeed about a new kingdom, a community of sons and daughters of God. But not just any aspect of this image. About the kingdom "coming". About that process, progress, setback, growth and decline, frost and sunlight, succession of seasons, good and evil intermingled, the human clutch and the letting go.

The reasoning went something like this: if the King image is replaced by the father image, then whatever replaces "kingdom" must be thought through once more. Or better, must be imagined anew. Let us overturn the imperial city, the walled kingdom, the control and pomposity and decrees and edicts and fear and life and death sentences. Let us give the world back to the imagination, so that we can once more imagine who we are — instead of having even that decreed for us. Let us stop implying that earthly rulers have anything substantial to offer the community of faith. Quite the opposite is the truth: earthly rule and whatever wobbly legitimacy it can claim stems from its likeness to the community of the beatitudes, its non-violence, compassion, and sense of justice.

Thus he started over. First, he led the people out of the city, even though it was the holy city. They stood together by the shore of a lake, near the open fields, where the casting of nets and the sowing of seed went on, the harvesting of wave and furrow.

And began.

The images of agriculture seem to have taken firmest hold on the hearers; they keep asking for explanations. Many of those so called "hearers" and "questioners" were of a later generation. So the parables have the charming character of dialogues with the future. Jesus tells a story, it ferments away in a vat of time, perhaps for a whole generation. Then, like a still scene in a primitive painting, time is erased. The future is painted in, the unborn get born. New difficulties have arisen in the churches, people come "to Jesus", perhaps to some holy elder or shepherd, asking for light. The light once struck is simply incorporated into the text: "this is what he meant in the first place."

The stories of Jesus are thus breathed on, kept fresh, reapplied to new needs. And we are reminded gently that a socratic dialogue is of the essence of learning, even though it is shouted across a canyon of time; the questions of one generation meet the wisdom of another.

"A sower went out to sow his seed . . ." With uneven results, to say the least. The word of truth falls by the roadside, among thorns, in stony places. The prodigality of God is put to the test, in the wastefulness and carelessness of natural process. Only here and there does the truth get a hearing.

The parable, it is implied, was not originally understood in this light. Indeed the case could be argued that it was only dimly understood at all. Telling stories — is this how to teach? Was the Lord being facetious, lightminded? Brought up on far different fare (the $2 + 2 = 4$ logic of the so-called real world, including the religious world), they were stumbling about bewildered.

But he was forthright, as usual.

Parables, he said in effect, cast a scrim between the mind and reality. They stop one short. They invite one to raise questions, they allow one to turn back, to shrug off so esoteric a "way." Indeed, these images of the rabbi are a kind of testing ground. Was there the insight, the suspicion that the truth lurked there in shadow, impelling one further? Did not new questions arise in the mind, when images were set in motion — images that were unfamiliar and perhaps threatening?

We are in deep waters here. A mood has been induced that seems at variance with the pastoral, easygoing scene of Jesus' teaching, out of joint also with the lovely images he evokes. It is as though a cloud passed over the sun, a chill fell on the air. Or as though the unresting, a single-minded soul of Christ could not bear to float in the shallow waters near shore, winning too easy an acquiescence from the untested, the self-deluded.

Not all will say, even with half a heart, "Thy kingdom come." Many have set up their own kingdom, themselves enthroned, their own violent acquisitive ego in command, their enemies their footstool, their injustice crying to heaven for vengeance.

Jesus cannot lose himself in the elusive perfections of a summer day. He is no idolater of ecology, at expense of the pain and darkness of human life, the limbo, the moral squandering of the soul's deep resources. Every ideal human scene, in his soul, summons up its own opposite. The cost of the "ideal" in this sense is a heavy one — the loss of a sense of the real. No, the reality of the world includes both the sower of seed, and the stony soul on which it comes to naught. This is not to be thought of as pessimism; it is rather the ground of a hope that is not deluded, not turned aside by the malice of sin.

In a sense, the images of sower and seed invite questions of this kind, questions which require much time to take form and to mature. What is the meaning of the parable? This is the query of a future generation, which has had to wrestle with the ambiguous response of the world to the word of God.

But the initial questions of the disciples should not be ignored. Why do you speak to them in parables at all?

Dualism, the cross, pain, inexplicable suffering, innocence under fire, the camp of the faithful and the host of the faithless, those who choose love and those who turn to the dark — What a cloud indeed has passed over the sun!

There are those who will cry out, "thy kingdom come". And there are those who will establish their own kingdom, on rocky soil, by roadsides, among thorns. For them, these will be their natural setting, their lethal ecology, their kingdom of this world, kingdom of the dead.

The method of parables is a serious one. It has no part with those who see the kingdom as a catch-all of half hearts, yea and nay sayers in the same breath, half idolaters, consulters of planets and animal guts, bowers and scrapers before money, bearers of arms, those who forge the credentials of the kingdom and would slip through into it, their pagan baggage intact. No, the game stops here.

Indeed, among his hearers on that faultless day, how many were named Stony Ground, Fruitless Wayside, Thorns and Briars! As events would prove, as life would test them, as the word on the summer air hardened and fell — a stone of scandal. As indeed, about this persuasive, silver-tongued (we would have said "charismatic") young preacher, a cloud of doom darkened. Could he be named Hundredfold, this driven one whom the word of truth impelled so far, so alone? It was a hundredfold burden, a hundred-weight, of horror — his harvest was death.

Jesus quotes Isaiah, in justifying his story telling. The quote is both curious and disturbing. It implies a waste, a waste of the truth, of the word of God, of life itself, a waste that indeed is taken in account, in the very saying of the truth: "That seeing they may not see, that hearing they may not understand." Isaiah's words are a somber footnote to the parable of the sower — and, in the mind of Christ, to the method of story telling itself.

Not a footnote we might have thought apt. One would look rather for a learned discourse on beauty, variety, chances taken, freedom invited, awakening of soul, the gentleness of the Lord, his playfulness, as his eye ranges over the world and knits together its signs and clues. Not at all.

As the roadside is there, other than the road, not meant for journeys, not pointing beyond — so is the loitering mind there, malingering, self indulgent, inert to the core. The birds of the air mock such a one. In their intrepid swiftness and greed, they pluck the truth from his hand and bear its kernel aloft. These small vultures are the thieves of indifference; they leave behind dead souls, dead on their feet.

Stony ground is there, in nature. We walk on it, we hew

granite from it, but only a fool would think to plant on it. Only some chance, a misdirected cast of the sower or a vagrant
wind, lodges the seed on rock. Such ground may be covered
with a thin veil of earth; it is all a deception. Indeed, the truth
may spring up for a time, but nature in this case works against
nature, element against element. The green shoots rise, a
mirage. The noon sun strikes them down like a sickle. No
roots, we say, nowhere to come from.

Then there is ground which bears an undergrowth, a tangle
of thorns and thistles. It is a metaphor for that thriving, knot-
ted, wounding jungle of motives and drives and devices we
call simply "the world". It plays safe, it grows close to the
ground; to anyone seeking a direct way, seeking a way out, it
is all but impenetrable. Nothing lofty, nothing fruitful, bitter
to the core, self armored, self contained. A cul de sac. Again,
some chance seed falls there, crawls toward a patch of sun,
thrives there for awhile. It grows straight up among the dis-
sembling; it seeks the upper air, an innocent in the jungle of
experience. But it is already captive; the thorn brake has cast
a net about the young plant; it is throttled in this living noose.

Why? The image is that of the virtuous loner, longing more
or less desperately to be 'different,' to listen and respond to
the truth. But the world, that tangled network of lies and lip
service, is simply too much. The solitary who would be godlike among the subhumans, is easily disposed of. You cut off
sustenance, cut off air and sun; transform solitude into utter
loneliness, a wasteland. And you have won. No crime is required; the truth isolated from the community of truth will
die of its own; it will simply give up.

Finally, the point and pith of the story, the fortunate seed;
whose "ecology of the spirit" is well ordained. Soil, air, sun.
Such a one hears, rejoices, responds. In such a one, the
kingdom comes; he/she is named Hundredfold.

Something of the story teller dwells in the story. Jesus is the
first of those in whom 'thy kingdom comes.' In him, the word
of the kingdom indeed fell upon good ground.

He is included in the parable, he transcends it. Which is to say, there are strong points to the story, there are neglected points to the story; necessarily, for no one parable can encompass the richness of Jesus' mind, the variety, the many ways he embraces the world. Thus if the good seed were conscious, it would suffer. If it were conscious, it would know that unless it die, it may not rise again. Text beside text, story against story, we gain those hints and starts and signs of Jesus, imagining the truth in truthful ways. We imagine the kingdom, which so far exceeds the sterile grasp of this world as to require the imagination of God himself to bring it to being, a second creation.

"The kingdom is like a grain of mustard, sown in a field." Prior scenes of sowing were largehanded, grand in their careless wide spread gesture. Now comes a more careful, even stingy sower, dealing out a seed so tiny as to be nearly invisible. We have a double paradox: the tiniest seed is sown in a field, one seed only. A hole is dug with bare hands, the single seed is deposited there and covered over. What are its chances? One in two, one in twenty, one in a hundred? No matter, the farmer will take his risks, let the vagaries of wind and weather do their worst.

The isolated seed, the isolation of a single truth, one aspect of the kingdom. Let us attend to it with all our hearts; the near invisibility of the kingdom of God in this world. That "kingdom," reduced to a speck, a mote — and underground! Its very existence, let alone its future, its growth, are matters of strict and bitter faith. We take it on his word — on the word of the farmer, who perhaps alone of all, knows the spot where the "tiniest of seeds" lurks, undergoes its sea and earth change. May survive, may not; may live, may rot away and be lost. We take our chance. We take our choice.

May I offer this gloss on the parable? It seems to me that as churches multiply, aggrandize, build to high heaven, accumulate goods and dish out services, train their clientele and secure their future, attract new members, enact in the sanctuary the restless fevers and icy chills of the culture — as all this motion, movement, buildup, fervent charade goes on, a kind of seismic shift takes place in the foundation stones of existence. The bones of the universe are shifting in their place. A new order is awakening from millenial sleep. The new creation stirs restively under this himalayan weight of "things", possessions, evidences, proofs, validations, come-ons, seductions, rapes, marriages of conveniences, whorings, hucksterings, this vast temple of idolatry and its massive appurtenances.

Take all of it, take it into account. Ponder its cultural analogies, the way in which the American church (for instance) is the sedulous ape, trained, fed, breeding, in captivity, on exhibit, the ape of America. Investing like America, rich like her, violent like her, diplomatically skilled like her — the spiritual arm and muscle of Gargantua.

Then come, let us be still for awhile. Come apart, to a remote country field. Let us stand here for awhile, in shadow. You will see. A strange rite is underway.

A farmer is crossing the field. His right hand is tenderly cupped, as though it held a bird's egg. His apron, with its pouch of seed, is quite empty. It is spring time, but the field is unplowed. There, in the middle point of his acre, the man kneels; with his left hand, he scoops up a handful of dirt, then another and another. He lowers his right hand into the earth, and deposits, with infinite care, a single, hardly visible seed. Then with both hands he tenderly replaces the mold, meticulously covers and smooths over the patch of earth. He stands for a moment, ruminatively. Then he goes off.

I thank Jesus for this parable. For the contrast it offers to the devouring madness of America, for the contrast it offers to the uncertain life, and certain death, of St. Gargantua — for these I give thanks. The contrasts speak to my heart, and warm my bones.

This is how it is today. The farmer of faith is a rather silent, even enigmatic, solitary, person. Says little, lives out of sight, out of mind. Looks on America, on American religion, with a certain sidelong detachment, as one who had more savvy than the savants, who has heard tell of a reaper, a grim one. Is a squatter on the land, which, in any case, is remote and unpromising, no bone of contention. And there, on his own, in solitary witness of the witlessness of things, he now and again, for reasons best known to himself, performs these symbolic rites, plants seeds, waters dry sticks, lives off the city dump, reconnoitres, takes soundings from old newspapers, leads the kind of shiftless, ambitionless existence that but for one thing, could be easily derided, ignored. But for this; on occasion he is capable of lightning flashes of humor, whipstock blows of wisdom.

But we were pondering one of his small home grown "liturgies," the planting of that mustard seed. So small a thing cast into so large a world! The gesture was, after all (among other things), a mime of his own existence, which seems to the majority of Americans unlikely, chancy, faintly absurd, harmless, and — though unattractive — in no sense to be taken seriously or found menacing.

Exactly. The kingdom. The tiny seed, out of sight, out of mind. Jesus Christ, buried in the world, level with the world, disposed of, done with, trodden upon, utterly lost.

When things are quite generally going mad, it is important to be a little mad. And above all else, to avoid like a plague the icy ultra-sanity of the powerful ones in church or state. As another farmer, Peter Maurin, put it: I don't mind being insane, but I insist on being crazy in my own way. Exactly: The opposite of officially sanctioned insanity, certified as sane, ponderous, pompous, functional, honorable, taken seriously by all the juridical and military and forensic machinery of the so-called sane — the opposite of all this, is a kind of grain-of-salt insanity, a mustard seed insanity, an insanity of good humor in a sea of starch and hogwash, an insanity of symbols and signs and small liturgies, a quasi insanity of the imagination. That skill of Jesus — it points in a quirky direction toward some neglected, despised, buried truth — which just might, if nurtured, held close, watered (even with tears) warmed, whispered to — might grow and flourish and make it!

When things and persons are stark, unraving, icy, logical, adamant against touch or human feeling, armored against tears, and when this so-called life proceeds under the most persuasive impenetrable sweet talking plausibility — when all this occurs as a matter of closed lips and dead eyes, a matter of nothing working for people, though it is said with a straight face that everything is constructed and set up and financed for people — when all this is going on, one had best start taking thought. Had best pause. And turn around. And run like hell in the opposite direction.

I mean this with all seriousness. The gospel injunction is simple: Flee. An opposite direction from the mad direction-less course of the culture, which in any case, in any conceivable outcome, whatever sop it concocts, is both murderous and suicidal — but most of all, is plain mad.

Flee. I mean by that, imagine yourself in another spiritual and, insofar as possible, another physical stance, one nothing at all like the lock step of the wooden soldiers. The opposite of such insanity — sanctioned and blessed as it is — is not sanity (as commonly understood, or misunderstood) but a small dose, a pinch, just a touch of a different insanity; or better still, a large dose of imagination.

Imagine it, put yourself there.

Now all this may be easily said, but true alternatives are hard come by. The culture swallows the counter culture, and calls it naked lunch; it is not even its main meal.

But the gospel is something else again. In some two millenia of assorted King Caesars, two bit and gold plated, no imperial stomach has been quite able to ingest this little book. Lucky we are, if we are literate. We may not yet be eaten . . . .

Come then to the country place, and witness (or enact) the parable of the seed that got lost. Everything about its fate is unlikely. It has practically (let us above all be practical) nothing to commend it; practically no future, practically no usefulness, no visibility, no beauty, no big sponsors. As yet, all but nothing. As of now.

It is in that vast loneliness, a next to nothingness, as though we ourselves were that tiny dust of seed (indeed we are) that we gain some sense of the kingdom of God, which is so far from having arrived on this earth, as to be in fact at any point, in any place, all but extinguished, all but wiped out. In us, that is. In us of no account, and all but obliterated in the world. The primary issue and insight here, I would think, is the near failure of the Lord's grace, outlook, sensibility, strength, in those who presumably comprise the kingdom.

Thus our image is not only in large and shocking contrast to the world; we are at a great distance from God. What we are is very near nothing at all; what we may be is so hypothetical, so dependent, so nearly unborn as in fact to comprise the void which lies between Him and ourselves.

In saying these things we are, strangely enough, speaking our hope. Thy kingdom come — even in us. The first heart beat, the first gracious sign of life, is your gift, no achievement of ours. Your kingdom come — even in the nettles and tares and entanglements of our violence, our demented self destroying obsessions.

Your kingdom come — even when we grant it (yourself) no room, no place, no honor, no voice, no attention.

Your kingdom come — even when we enlist slavishly in the imperial projects, building the kingdom of this world, the kingdom of death. Your kingdom come — the indivisible speechless seed that makes no big claims, works no magic; but would, if given room and place, heal our inhumanity, render us sane, bold, imaginative, hopeful. Heal us.

we ourselves were that tiny dust of gold flashed we are) that we gain a more sense of the kingdom of God, which is so far from having arrived on this earth . . . to be in fact at any

## Your Will Be Done On
## Earth As It Is In Heaven

The will of the son, the will of the father. Two wills perfectly conjoined, we were taught as children (and later, when we
presumably were no longer children).

Experience, and a closer reading of the new testament,
make one cringe when that word "perfect" is hauled out.
What a neat Greek universe! How we admire the clockwork,
hearkened to its perfect timing and tick! the will of father and
son perfectly (!) interlocking, gear on gear.

Then life comes along, and questions arise. If one is lucky,
one opens the bible again, and discovers that the teachers
were not entirely wedded to the text. Because what one reads
there is perilously distant from perfectionism, a little closer to
one's day by day mucking through.

This holy son was no closed parenthesis, his life among us
no "given," no game. He did not know the end in the beginning. Even the theologians are willing to grant him what they
called experiential knowledge, though they hedge and fudge
about and take back half of what they granted — as though
they were constructing him out of their own heads, instead of
listening and learning and being silent, as was the method of
the wise, the mystics or peasants, or Matthew or John. Still,
the gospel survives them all.

Let us start like this. If an image, figure, metaphor, is to be
helpful, it has to be reasonably faithful to the realities it sets
up, or borrows from. Thus if Jesus talks about himself as

73

son, and God as father, it would seem that the last thing on his mind is a "perfectly conjoined" arrangement. Nothing in biology or the human spirit or the experience of fathers and sons would support such a notion. Neither, let us say with a sigh of relief, does the gospel.

What we are offered under that image is something other than an icy static final form. One is not to conjure the impossible image of two persons side by side, hands joined, locked in an ancient ice floe, embalmed forever. From one point of view, these dead images are perfect, perfectly preserved; they stay together, their forms suggest they pray together. This may even be the kind of "perfect" god-human image we truly look for.

The reality is something else. Good sons don't get along very well with their fathers; that is, if they have good fathers. Fathers who respect their sons (and recall their own fathers) don't look for such a parody; they look for equals, intelligences, mutual respect, plain speech, not discipleship but equity, the love expressed in level look. So with the sons: they know it is a mark of death to be "in the old man's power"; they must strike free, become someone on their own, take on the world by taking on their father.

This is something of the reality the image of Jesus tries to offer. Fathers and sons are at peace in the house, only as long as the sons are children. But neither father nor son, if each has a sense of reality, would call these the best years, or fail to look further. One day all that peace, tenderness, inequality, dependence, prodigality, nurturing, all those smiles and tears, the mysterious bonding, that hand in this — all this must go, explode. Then we have something close to a revolution — or in religious terms, a reformation. The son draws up his version of the universe, pinpoints his place in it. And he nails it to the front door.

When we come to apply this scene to Jesus and the father, we must go gingerly. We are pondering an image, not a literal fact of life. Jesus and the father are not two related males walking the world. "My Father" is an image of a God who "imagines," bespeaks, conceives, another, called "my Son". And the son in time joins our ranks and walks the earth, truly one of us. So we must be aware of the strength as well as the limits of our image father-son.

Still, I am pleading for a better balance. When we pull Jesus down to our human size (miniscule) we are destroying the balance. And when we introduce an empyrean perfection in the father-son image, we are wreaking a like havoc with the uneasy truth. Somewhere in the middle, we walk, on a kind of hot high wire. If Jesus could pray, "Your will be done on earth as it is in heaven," he prayed it with such overmastering dread, terror, sense of death invading his bones, that the blood started on his brow, a bloody death sweat before his hour. The truth should give our bloodless perfectionism pause. Go slow, only fools rush in here.

When we seek to understand the words of Jesus, we had best look at his life, its whole course, its outcome. This is not easy; we have been, on the one hand, conned too often in affairs human and divine; good word, bad conduct; or big promise, faint resolve. On the other hand, pseudo-heroes litter the landscape, including religious ones. They offer the "fast food" of instant salvation, a trashy, pitiful magic that, to say the least, doesn't work, doesn't even persuasively deceive. Living examples of moral consistency are few indeed. Whose words and works join hands today in a way that gives joy, let alone makes sense to us?

All this turning to the past! Is that what we do when we give attention to Jesus? Do we indulge a sacred nostalgia? I think there is something more to be said. Apart from all else, the quest for a higher will, a higher goodness, a sanction superior to our social contract and secular covenants — this is a powerful antidote to the poisonous anomie of America, that cutting of the tap root, which the culture wreaks on us. Being in conflict with God cannot be so bad a thing. After all, the fight means at least that we come from someone's loins, that we graduated out of nurture and caring, into some measure of responsibility, stewardship, clumsy and embattled though we are.

Your will be done. What a storm those calm words turn away from — at least for a time! We are not to think the calm will endure; any more than that the storm will go away if one looks elsewhere. Jesus of course was no sleight of hand artist; he taught us calm words which have the virtue of cooking up a furious clash — or at least of taking it into account. Indeed such a prayer can only be said, in optimum (which is to say, in fact, pessimum) circumstances; at the hour of death.

Again, I have recourse to the experience of Jesus. It was one thing to commend certain words of petition to his friends, when they addressed the father of all. It was quite another thing to test out the words, or like words, in his own flesh. Then "our father . . . your will be done" becomes a prelude to torment: "My father, if it be possible, let this cup pass from me." It was not possible; the cup did not pass. It was impossible, things could not be otherwise. So he died, in so inhuman a fashion (surely one of the most terrible deaths of all our savage history). This impossibility, this iron fate, this closed will descending like a closed fist — this simply tore the image father-son to pieces. "My God, my God" — still "my", but where has the Father gone?

For this reason death, which is called a moment of truth, is also the moment of the truest prayer — "your will be done." Now there is no more talk of father and son; the metaphor which for all his life, had worked, is abandoned. At the moment of death language fails and falls away. From one point of view, an unutterable tragedy; from another, the highest achievment of all those images, metaphors, those cunning, genius-laden devices by which he attained sense and sanction in the world. Only to be transcended, to fail triumphantly. This is why he dies in a great silence. Those of us who are fortunate at that hour will have a friend or two at our side; but if the friends are wise, they will content themselves with a gesture of grief and compassion. In silence they will solace our hour; and rehearse their own.

We have suggested that the image of the father was a development of the image of the kingdom of God. This was by no means meant to evacuate the new image of the massive social meaning which the ancient one held. To do so would, among other things, derange the Lord's prayer out of all recognition. Your will be done. It was not only a personal struggle of two mature wills that is acted out in the gospel. It is also a struggle of historic forces, universal, titanic in scope. The will of God is the burden of nations, a ferule of iron on stiff necks.

Who dares say this today? The churches are bent like a covey of children over a play pen, a touchie-feelie religion that in reality touches hardly anything or anyone in the real world. The prophets who cry aloud are effectually and finally silenced; or they are simply ignored. The culture, the political system, have the perfect consistency and immobility of a county morgue; every corpse in its proper place, drugs, chill, moral inertia, observed law, admirable order.

Meantime, of course, there is a back room to the establishment. There the powerful concoct their plans, parcel out the earth, experiment on the living and the dead, make and unmake history. God? The will of God? A living God, observant of the world, providential, just, wrathful? The notion is alive as, say, the "contents" of those icy chambers. God is like the dead, a casualty of life today; that is all. And the churches, who bless and bury the dead with a kind of horrid dispatch, bless and bury him as well. No more admirable arrangement could be conceived.

"On earth as it is in heaven." We are not to think of two worlds, a geographic dualism. But still, two moral universes, two "kingdoms", so to speak. For a time, that is — as long as time lasts; or more properly, as long as the reign of sin and death "abounds". Still, a promise joins the two, earthly city and celestial, kingdom of light and darkness, reign of sin, reign of love. That promise, his "will," joins the two; indeed, it interpenetrates the world with hope, even now.

And at the end of things, the most wonderful images offered to us, are those of unity, a marriage. A bride and bridegroom, a celestial city descending in an act of love, on the earthly. A tree, "whose leaves are for the healing of the nations." And finally, the city.

> The people of the earth will walk by (the glory of God), and the kings of the earth will bring their wealth. The gates of the city will stand open all day; they will never be closed, because there will be no night there. The greatness and wealth of the nations will be brought into the city. . .

In spite of all, in spite of death as a stated way of life, in spite of the city morgue and its sinister guardians, none of this triumph or claim is definitive, a final form or word.

One is staggered before the power of the contrary hope, the calm with which these final images of life and harmony are offered. Has God joined the intoxicated pipers and dreamers in the market place? It all seems something like a druggie's nirvana. Obedient, life affirming kings reign, uncontaminated wealth gleams in the city of God, the nations are healed of their crimes, their torture, their defamation, all slave camps are closed, all kangaroo courts sternly silenced, the poor are rewarded for the injustices they have endured, the rich reproved for their crimes. It is enough to stop the heart.

We have sunk so low, we can scarcely imagine, any longer, a simply human order of things. All our lives we struggle against an apparently irresistible tide of social savagery, insanity. Who of us can name a single nation state which observes the rule of law, with regard even to virtuous dissidents, which renounces war, which protects the innocent, which is a just steward of the earth? Out of the depths we cry to you.

On earth, as in heaven — your will.

The prayer will be answered, rigorously, gloriously. Because God is God; that in the first instance. But also, because we pray, because we labor and suffer in measure, because we walk humbly in his way.

In our bitter world, good intentions are very nearly

fruitless. I mean intentions that never touch ground, or that do so rarely, whose proper level is weightlessness, upper air. When will we come to prefer the imperfect act to the perfect and pure intention?

It is in some such way that the "will of God" ought to be regarded; a good intention that, in Jesus, touched ground. A glorious idea; and immediately in trouble!

The trouble is ourselves. The trouble is, the church. The trouble is apostasy, crusades, hatred of minorities, fear of the variety and chutzpah which were (in the order of intention) once and for all approved in the act of creation; were approved once more, in the order of history and culture, by the Incarnation of God's son. Not only approved, but grounded, sealed.

Of course we dissembled. Of course we had second thoughts, and third, and so on; and armed ourselves against women and gays and blacks and native Americans and so on; our second thoughts concerning the "second creation" are endless, a bloody rout.

But at least we know; the stigma is on us, the stigma of the divine. That footprint of the ascending Jesus which, legend tells us, lies on the stone of an eastern mountain, is imprinted on our stony hearts. We cannot quite erase it, we cannot quite be done with what once manifestly happened to us, within us.

It could be argued that we were worsened by this intemperate exposure to the divine. The argument is a familiar one. We heard another version of it often during the Vietnam years: by resisting the war, you succeeded only in prolonging the war. Prosit. In the case of Jesus, an interesting objection indeed, the divine can only worsen an already bad situation; worse, wounds it beyond remedy. Be perfect as your heavenly father is perfect. Come now! Your will be done on earth as in heaven. Come now!

We seem to be dealing with two versions of human nature; total depravity, total goodness. The lapsarians, the optimists club. I hesitate to present Jesus as the victimized evidence that my human frame is "improved" or "worsened" because he walked the earth. Indeed it seems to me he walked, not so much the earth, as the high wire we had reference to before. Something like this; he identified passionately with human life, especially in its defeated, rejected outcasts. On the other hand, he kept a certain distance from the involvement we like to think of today as "relevant", or in some related weasel way. He was supremely, disdainfully, firmly irrelevant — to the point that he died rather than be assimilated. After all this, it seems like our sour grapes to make him historically responsible for our violence, our murder, our bombs. To these latter, he would not only be "irrelevant" today; he would be in active fierce resistance.

Obedience. The need to obey. The majestic, exalting aspects of this creatureliness, as exemplified in Jesus. Then too, the depraved and corrupting aspects, as exemplified in the modern state, the lockstepping minds that create it, that obey it.

The obedient being: imagine the world as a physical order of powers and submissions, of interlaced support and soul and dominance. The ethical order, the political order (at its highest) is conceived of in a like way: choirs of angels, orders of authority, mediators of the divine. It worked for a long time; from the Greeks to the Middle Ages. But it could be argued that Jesus came, not to reinforce such a world system, but to disrupt it. Just as it could be argued that the dead end of the Greek universe was the Nazi iron box. Which has by no means been destroyed — by a war which only succeeded in expanding the box, building more rooms, tiger cages, prisons, until the box is now a kind of Universal Western Detention Center.

As far as Catholic priests are concerned, it was a long-lived polite supposition that, in America, the will of God could never collide with the will of the state. It was a kind of "state church" that so interpreted (one had best say defamed or defused) the gospel. We were kept in line, which was humorously referred to as the "long black line." But no one pointed out to us the quasimilitary character of all this, how perilously we were near to aping the civic lockstep. Obey, Obey! It was the will of God, they said; but how useful that will was to Caesar (and is)!

They call us utopian because we want the killing of people to stop. Immediately, here and now. As God's manifest will. As our way of declaring, ashamed indeed, late indeed — that such questions never should have arisen; questions like "is it legitimate to kill", or, "how many can we kill, and still be bona fide Christians?" We said, shame! Stop it! Not one more death. And that was, and is, the scandal.

## Give Us This Day Our Daily Bread

In a prayer which beats around no bushes, and wastes no words, the repetition of "day . . . daily" must be accounted remarkable. (The text is a vexed one, but the one we follow is ancient and hallowed.)

The attention given to bread in the gospel is surely remarkable. One might at this point read and ponder the majestic sonorities of John's chapter 6; beginning with the miraculous feeding of the five thousand, and proceeding to a discourse on truth as bread, bread as truth; then too, the account of the eucharist in all four evangelists.

The transcendent parts of the Lord's prayer are finished with: "your name be hallowed . . . your will be done . . ." Now we pray for ourselves; we draw the Father's attention to our needs; needs that might otherwise be considered beneath godly concern. But no, it is Jesus who points not only to the dignity of our daily round, but also to the father's attentiveness; indeed, such attention confers that dignity on us.

Possibly it is not in the loftiest service of the truth that one claims to pray easily, lightheartedly. That one not as they say, sweat over form and substance; and over meaning as well. We have little or no evidence that God attends to prayers whose image is that of the self justified "people of God", to their requests (with a certain high cynicism, pride of place) for things they already possess, in superabundance.

I am suggesting that we, author and readers of these words,

are not in a position beyond challenge, scrutiny, bitter critique, as we presume to say the words of this prayer.

It is properly, exactly, a petition of the hungry, for the hungry, to be uttered by lips habitually deprived of what they petition for. We obviously stand outside that circle. Who of us then can utter these words, literally asking for bread, bread of this day, and utter the words in good faith, when our larders are full, and our bank books hardly empty?

It is terrible to have a prayer commended to us, whose words we can utter in good faith only if we take thought most painfully, alter our lives, shift our values, resign our ill gotten prosperity, stop creating hunger, cease taxpaying for death, open our eyes to the suffering of the world, put our flags at half mast (or in moth balls), lay down our secret arms, become troublesome to the principalities.

Meantime, a terrible vision must assail us. The vision of a vast chorus of the neglected, hungry, deprived, assaulted, pillaged, tortured peoples of this world, a chorus of furies and judges and victims, surrounding us, just beyond our walls and windows and guarded acres. They repeat night and day, a terrible insistent clamor, the prayer: give us this day our daily bread. They drown out the cacophany of our trashy TV, they silence the sounds of dolce vita around the dining tables, they invade our nurseries and bedrooms and churches, they give the lie to every lying politician, every chattering preacher in his pulpit.

They repeat the prayer interminably, they call out, the just ones described by Jesus, "to the father, night and day."

And they are never heard.

It is important to say this, they are never heard. The bread does not arrive; neither in the beaks of birds, nor in the ample baskets descending from on high. Their bitter fate turns the words of Jesus around; they ask for bread; he gives them a stone.

We cannot escape the scene; it is a scene of judgement. The truth is not merely that we lie outside the petition, that our possessions exclude us. More than that. We actually deny the petition a hearing.

In the miracle of bread multiplied, Jesus dramatizes the prayer in its full round. That is to say, he anticipates the need ("where can we buy enough food to feed all these people?"). Then he simply responds — giving them, on that day, their daily bread.

The extraordinary, the dramatic, the miraculous intervenes. He wishes to give a kind of concentrated version, parable, image, of the utterly ordinary. The miraculous turns our gaze toward the quotidian. What the earth brings to pass in its circle of seasons and growth, of rain and sun, Jesus does abruptly, here and now. The same thing. The miracle is a transcendent gift; a reminder of the process of the good earth; no more. The ample gift, the baskets of food, the "more than enough", are reminders of a simple fact; when left alone, when nurtured, when loved, the earth is enough.

The problem is not "too many people". This should be stated once and for all. The phrase "population explosion" must be seen, in the light of creation and providence, as a military metaphor, a metaphor of violence. People explode, granted. They explode, in the immemorial way of flesh and bone, when they are bombed, napalmed; also when the goods and services of the earth are ripped off under their feet. Two wars, the war of deprivation and material misery; and then the wars "employing ever more destructive and indiscriminate weapons". But really, the two are one; a war on life, a war against community. A war against the future itself, and the children.

"Population explosion" indeed. An abstraction which hides the true intent of violence. A problem wrongly stated. Abortion, slum housing, legitimate war, world hunger, capital punishment.

Question: When do wrong questions arise?

When people have been wronged. When the people who wrong other people believe they have a right to do so. And make a rite of their right.

Question: What rite?

I mean the rite of war, and all its bloody analogues; fast death, slow death; abortion and war on the one hand, smoldering hunger on the other. But always death, the main drive and scope and method — from technology to diplomacy.

Question: What is to be done about all this?

Right the wrongs. At least to this degree: that one's complicity with death is cut back and back, until it stands harmless, at the vanishing point. You cannot serve two masters, life and death.

Question: What do you mean by the "militarized imagination"?

I mean that you cannot pray to the God of abundance for bread, in good faith, and offer the neighbor a stone, in bad faith. Especially since a stone cannot really be offered, it can only be flung; military method once more.

Our daily bread.

Since the petition has no sensible meaning for some of us, we would like to "get on with" some "meaning" — snatching at some way to make the words include us. This is a spiritual method, commonly known as the "Blessed End Run of Bad Faith".

But I have suggested another way, which I think is somewhat closer to the integrity of Jesus. First, let us admit that we cannot say the words as though they described our lives or spoke for real needs. But let us not stop there, malingering on the doorstep of cynicism, that limp intertia so dear to the self-willed helpless, whose skill is making the better the enemy of the good. No. Admitting that we lie outside the prayer (and indeed fear to stand in its emaciated circle) let us at least make it a little less improbable that the prayer be heard at all.

Reduce as they say in the old ethics books, the "obex", the stone in the path, the obstacle; not the obstacle to miracles, but to the simple providential fruitful course of the world. Get out of the way of the universe, stop polluting its harvests, wasting its fruits, forever bending plowshares into swords. In sum, paying a head tax to support the beheaders.

Those in possession of the earth, who are troubled by the preceding remarks, might consider the healing properties of civil disobedience. Our usual game is playing providence to our own interests and calling it divine providence; a closed system, the checks and (bank) balances of hell.

But now and again, as tattered wards of the state, some of us appear to ourselves in a new light. (We break the law, let us say, in defense of those deprived of daily bread; for war is the iron handed poor master, the dispenser of stones, not bread.) But say we are summarily locked up. Suddenly, we are a deprived people. We taste (only just taste, are not really surfeited on) the breadlessness of unfreedom. A whiff of death is around us; not an overpowering stench, just a momentary breath on the stale air. We are landlocked, unproductive, unskilled, useless, the third estate of the third world. There is contempt for our book learning, we are for a time useless, parasites, subjects of punishment.

Of course relief lies ahead, our plight is by no means to be compared seriously with that of the breadless peoples. Only a hint, a lagniappe, a taste. But the petition does come alive, we eat more thoughtfully, gratefully. Give us bread, daily, today.

Someone who gives bread away today is roughly in the same shoes as someone who speaks the truth. Both are in danger of being certified as insane, or jailed as troublemakers, or simply put to death. The vital nexus between bread and truth was explored by Jesus, who saw the two as mutual symbols and realities, the soul hungering for one, the body for the other. (John 6.)

Truth is to the spirit as bread is to the body. But what a diet of junk bread and junk truth most of us are on, most of our lives! The one who eats such bread dies of it; it is the other face of the Lord's promise.

World enough for all.

I think this is a kind of preamble of faith. Bread enough for all. The planetary system, so intricately and cunningly devised, favors all. I think we cannot believe in God, or follow Jesus, without coming to some such understanding. Otherwise we are constantly captive to the mad butchers and tinkers, for whom greed, violence and lust are the cardinal virtues.

Most Americans would like to have the Pentagon and the welfare state, the bread basket and bomb turret both full, death and life feeding at the same table, wrestling it out on the same battlefield. We dream of some demonic marriage between Christ and Baal. We love healthy bouncy children, we regretfully slaughter children. We want a stake in both sides of the Great Divide, the chasm set up between heaven and hell. Spiritually such an effort is absurd; the contradictions literally tear us apart; schizoid, a fair image of those who dwell not in both places, but simply in hell.

The bread of justice. The bread of truth. The bread of affliction. The bread (finally) of the kingdom. What resonances are attached to a simple loaf! It contains our history; broken, it releases, like a host of singing birds, our destiny.

They bribe the starving, the afflicted, the gulag prisoners, with a meager ration of bread; enough to sustain a feeble life, not enough to reach or vault over the wall. Meantime, threats of cutting even that frayed life line, keep most prisoners captive to untruth, to silence, impel many of them to betray their fellows . . . And who could be so foolish as to cast blame on such tried and tortured spirits?

The analogies of all this to the bread of life should give us pause. It is possible to put Christians on so thin a ration of the truth, that the bread of life becomes a kind of prolongation of dying, a prison ration, a slow poison. It is not enough, as Jesus shows, to offer us a "bread of life" that is bereft of the truth, the words of life. In southern Africa, I preached in churches where the word "apartheid" had not been mentioned for a generation. The bread of life was moldering in the cupboard; the dead were feeding the dead.

. . . . it follows then that if someone eats the Lord's bread and drinks from his cup in a way that dishonors him, such a one is guilty of sin against the Lord's body and blood. So everyone should examine himself first, and then eat the bread and drink from the cup.

For if one does not recognize the meaning of the Lord's body when he eats the bread and drinks from the cup, he brings judgement on himself in eating and drinking. That is why many of you are sick, and others have died. If we would examine ourselves first, we would not come under God's judgement.

But we are judged and punished by the Lord, so that we shall not be condemned together with the world. (1 Cor. 11)

No more powerful nexus could be drawn between the bread of truth and the bread of life. Judgement, recognition are the main theme here. The breaking of the bread is a "recognition scene". We discern in faith the body of the Lord; just as elsewhere, in the world, at work, in families, we discern, judge, take account of, the body of the Lord.

How can we make the eucharist, and still make war, prepare for war, justify murder? The bread should stick in our throat, the cup burn us like an acid.

No more terrible lack of discernment could be imagined, no more terrible judgement on ourselves, than the decision to kill others, at some government's iron behest. We have learned to distrust them in almost all else, how take their word on this murderous enterprise?

A true understanding of modern government (or ancient), of the strict limits of their claim on citizens, as well as an illustration of their treatment of virtuous dissidents — it begins at the eucharist. Begins here for believers, who "examine themselves first, (and do) not come under God's judgement." Surely one element of this self examination, this scrutiny of the community and individual soul, is the stance of the community before civil powers. How ignore this? The death announced and enacted here, is the death of a criminal, a dissident under capital sentence. It was another instance, by no means the first, of the state's "war on the saints".

What a hideous deformation of the eucharist! The community, a thoughtless jumble of virulent secular power, good tribute payers to Caesar, ignorant complaisant priests, a laity leveled off to a mute sheep faced citizenry! Truly in such cases, the world has invaded the sanctuary, the community will "be condemned together with the world."

One thinks of the captivation of the eucharist by the American ethos. The spirit of the modern world, that fusion of violence and duplicity and imperial dreams of grandeur, all this cohabits quite amicably with the ecclesiastical power. No argument, a secular covenant quite satisfactory to both sides. Sunday comes, both sides settle back; masses in the White House, war all week in Vietnam. Ten years of such pseudo-eucharists were enough to invalidate, for a generation, the words of eucharist, even while they starkly animated the "condemnation together with the world" announced by Paul.

Christmas 1977 at the Pentagon. Certain Christians entered the chapel area, and during the service, rose to speak of the blasphemy; presuming to conduct worship in that place of calculated death. Purportedly it is the day of Christ's birth. In reality it is the day of the Bomb.

The wicked one will appear, who is destined to hell. He

will oppose everything we worship and everything we consider divine. He will put himself above all, and will even go in and sit down in God's temple and claim to be God . . . The mysterious wickedness is already at work . . . The wicked one will come with the power of Satan, and will perform all kinds of miracles and false signs and wonders, and use every kind of wicked deceit on those who will perish. They will perish because they did not welcome and love the truth so as to be saved. For this reason, God sends the power of error to work in them so that they believe what is false. The result is that all who have not believed the truth, but have taken pleasure in sin, will be condemned. (2 Thes. 2)

These Christians, who believe one is not allowed to break the bread and squander the blood of children, even by intention, by preparing "new contingencies" (which are always verified, there belongs the true intent), these Christians arose to say such things as Paul had said.

A great ugly clamor arose. They were invaders, trouble-makers, they refused to others the rights they claimed for themselves . . . And in the midst of all, while the military and police were arresting the unwelcome ones, the voice of the minister could be heard like a buzzard over a battlefield: "No one in the world desires peace more sincerely than the military."

"If we would examine ourselves first, we would not come under God's judgement . . ."


Make bread, not war.

"This day, give us our daily bread." The cry is a terrible one, a cry of injustice unrepaired. It should be so understood. It is not the pallid whimper of a sated people for a tasteless supernal "wonder bread." Properly understood, the petition is one with the mysterious scene of the opening of the seals, in the book of Revelation. The four horsemen have been re-leased; time and this world have done their worst. But there is unfinished business in the world; judgement is yet to come.

I saw underneath the altar the souls of those who had been killed because they had proclaimed God's word and had been faithful in their witnessing. They shouted in a loud voice, Almighty Lord, holy and true, how long will it be until you judge the people of earth and punish them for killing us? (Rev. 6: 9-10)

This is the "other side" of that companionable, amiable, milksop rite we have made of the Eucharist. A scene of judgement; the judgement which troublesome Christians of our own day announced in the midst of the pentagonal temple of death. How long, O Lord?

A scene of the end, but not quite of the end. Both bread and justice have been denied; it was almost a definition of time itself, deprivation, death, injustice. The great yawn of the beast is wide as the jaws of hell. The power of evil, of death multiplied, of the perfect coherence of the imperial method, is contemptuously victorious. Indeed, "victorious" seems almost too immodest a word to describe what has occurred. The beast would wave the description aside negligently; it was all so easy, it was like surrounding a drug dive in the dead of night, taking the comatose addicts captive. No need of casualties, bloodletting; the casualties, morally speaking, had occurred long before.

The sanctuaries? They fell too.

"Fell" again: a military word. Let us speak rather of a drift toward the beast, an atmosphere, a complacency. The sanctuaries fell; say rather they had been captive to the demonic for a long time. Their "fall" was a mere announcement of a *fait accompli*. It was devoid of interest, even for the world. And for the somnolent Christians, the announcement of a "new governance" had no interest whatsoever. They shifted and turned in sleep. And this was hell.

The breaking of seals is the breaking of bones. It is the breaking of the code, the breaking of both the cognito and the incognito of Christ. We know him in the breaking of the bread; but this cannot be merely announced here, without being tested elsewhere. We are indeed tested and found wanting, elsewhere; and this is the judgement.

"When you do these things, remember me." For some, this call to remember is an exercise in nostalgia. We do not remember, we dismember. We would like to dwell in time as though we were in nirvana. We would like to live in the world as though the world were America; true blue, my country right or wrong. We would like to eat the bread of remembrance as though it were the lotus of amnesia. We would like literally to "eat" Christ, to destroy him like a pagan hero, whose heart would heal us of the pain of the world; to "absorb" him into the tainted secular dream: my country 'tis of thee.

We are in dread of that ragged human figure, that vagrant one. So we cosset him in the petty robes of divinity-to-order, an infant of Prague, fit for the infants. This of course misses the point both of the divine and the human. Missing the point: it is almost a summation of religion today. Come to me, all you who would miss the point.

And who dares sit at this table, who has not shared the labors, from planting through hoeing and watering, the sweats and dreads, locusts, droughts, tares, animal appetites on the loose — and then the harvest?

In the early '60's, scandal attended efforts to break the eucharistic bread in New York homes. I was even placed by superiors under a kind of house arrest at the time, for reported violations of church law. The crime can be simply stated: we wanted to meet with friends around a table and celebrate the Lord's death in simple American English.

Yesterday's scandal is today's cliche. With a difference. Many of those who attended the new liturgies in those days began to say to themselves (somewhat as though we were dishing up a novel), "How interesting; and what's next?" It being of the essence of this novelty that it quickly wear out, lose its fascination for spoiled minds.

There was in fact, no "next". In fact, in principle. So our friends simply walked out on it all.

If we had been prepared to serve a "next course" of say, matzos and cokes, the exodus might have been delayed. But some of us had an absurd notion: we were not in the novelty or sideshow business at all. So we simply hastened an exodus that was inevitable after all. Those walking out of house liturgies met their opposite numbers, those walking out of the dead churches; the post-Christians converged from both directions. Better, the post-Christians had never tasted Christianity. What had occurred was not a failure of nerve, or a failure of Latin, or least of all, a failure of the sacraments. It was the death of faith itself.

## Forgive the Wrongs We Have Committed, as We Forgive the Wrongs We Have Done to Others

And there follows immediately a comment of the Lord; "If you forgive others the wrongs they have done you, your father in heaven will also forgive you. But if you do not forgive the wrongs of others, then your father in heaven will not forgive the wrongs you have done."

The Lord refers forgiveness immediately to the Father.

Moreover, as in other instances where he means to shock, paralyze, upset tradition, open vast horizons, even bring on a kind of trauma — upsetting the old in favor of the (virtually) untried new — in this instance also, Jesus tests his teaching first of all in his own flesh. So he says from the cross: Father forgive them, they do not know what they do.

Something more than altruism is at work here. Jesus is not merely stepping aside from the messy business of crime and reconciliation. How can he imaginably do so, when the greatest of crimes will be committed against himself?

Something more indeed. As in the parables of forgiveness, the Father is invoked, in order to assert a right order.

Which is to say, this matter of forgiveness is crucial, it goes to the heart of things; it must be referred to the creator himself.

The one who refuses to forgive is equivalently a murderer. Jesus beats around no bushes. The unforgiving one, bent on revenge and self justification, is the disruptor par excellence.

He extends the original sin in time, invokes it, takes it to heart, renews it, makes it, again and again, hideously original.

There is one way to erase the taint, to stop its infection, to reduce its malevolent hold on human kind. Forgive. And the cycle is broken.

Let us hear a story about this matter, a wildly improbable one; perhaps this is the only way of touching this wildly improbable matter of human reconciling, the voluntary wiping out of offense, the putting aside of all the clamorous persuasive thoughts of restitution, of degrees of guilt, and (most difficult and obscure of all) one's responsibility as to the moral improvement, rehabilitation, of the offender. All are put aside.

The story, it should be noted, does not concern a crime of violence. The forgiveness of murder, a plea in that direction, is quite literally and ironically another story. In that matter, we have the simple account of the last hour of Jesus. That is our parable, our glory and gift, for all time.

But to our story: Jesus tells about a crime against property. We are not to miss the humor. Property, possessions, are such a deadly humorless subject among humans! Property, property! The vultures around a death bed, the mask falling away from the old tycoon. Or the aged rich thief, who has pillaged the poor of the earth, and refurbished his dead soul with gifts of dimes to urchins — one could go on and on. Why indeed does the amassing of money freeze the soul? . . .

In our story, God will poke a little fun at the follies of mammon. (Mt. 18, 23)

The Father of all is, it appears, something like an American billionaire. The sun seldom sets on his kingdom. He can therefore be a bit careless about his holdings, imprudent even; a million here, a careless accounting there, down wind, up wind — why should Croesus be a crease-brow?

But one day, an accounting is called for. The lord of the manor descends on his holdings, calls for the ledgers.

Zounds! The books are opened, the red ink flares up. His steward is a crook; in arrears moreover, to the tune of some MILLIONS OF DOLLARS!

Confusion, confounding. A scene worthy of the mordant genius of Dickens or Defoe. In the whole kingdom and realm and glittering history of Tycoonery, what greater crime could be summoned up? Our tycoon, our benefactor, has been flummoxed, bamboozled, cuckolded, plainly had. A million here, a million there indeed — but this is larceny approaching the national debt!

The scene is like a Wall Street still-life. You could hear a nickel roll on rubber. The delinquent is dragged in. He has lost everything but his cool. He sinks to the floor. This crook, this petit-tycoon, is quite as the grave. Only his weather eye is agleam, like silver in a back pocket.

He kneels there on the floor, he lets it all sink in. Crime? What crime? He learned all he knows at the feet of his benefactor. There he spent his happiest hours. Emulating. Admiring, envying a little, reaching out a little, testing the waters. A croupier gainfully employed. He reached, he raked it all in, and that was that.

Hence his smile.

Let's be reasonable, kind sir. If it's so admirable to be Big, what harm is it being a little less big? If grand larceny is petted and stroked and rewarded by the world, why should petty larceny be crushed?

The learned scholars miss something rather consistently, I think. In the story, Jesus enters into the messy matter of the Mixed Motive. This is scandalous indeed, that the savior would so picture the heavenly father — biting his finger nails with vexation because one of His Own is guilty of being — what? A little like the Old Amasser?

In any case, you sense the dilemma: The Lord Of All, a bit short on surveillance, a bit remiss in his ledgers, takes counsel within himself. And his recusant servant, undoubtedly also a bit of a recidivist, wriggles and squirms at his feet.

We must not keep him there overlong. On the other hand,

we must not bring him to his feet too quickly. Let us see.

Our Leader ponders things.

Then; yes. I will wipe the ledgers clean.

Thus at one stroke, I accomplish several designs: I offer first of all, a valuable lesson in theology. Mortals who now and then are victims of petty losses, of missing pfennings, cannot but take heart and react openhandedly, when they reflect on the Matter of the Missing Millions. Thus I establish a kind of ikon of supernal conduct, upon which all may meditate and be comforted.

Also: my solution has a further object. In forgiving the top man (doubtless this fellow has a crew of squalid companions below stairs), I stop all investigation here, on the instant. Of me. Let us say it; of me.

Then up fellow, on your feet. I forgive you, I restore you. O don't thank me, thank your heavenly father, your stars, the charismatic movement, and my daily meditations on the karma, on ahimsa, on the great vow of the Buddha. Let me confess, I had considered for a long moment shipping you to the gulag for life, you and your misfortunate spouse, your too-numerous brats. But I have hearkened to my voices. I hear only the hymning of the spheres. Arise. And get out.

And the delinquent stumbles to his feet, choked with gratitude.

Would that our story could end here, on so Christian a note.

But no. Our friend makes his bewildered way out of the presence of this blinding munificence. He can hardly see. He hardly cares. He is careful however, to convey even in his dishevilment, the right note; an image of repentance unalloyed.

He is now outside the throne room. He has drawn his sleeve away from his fevered brow.

And whom do his eyes rest upon in that moment? A lowly stable hand, a mote in the eye of good fortune.

The fellow, he instantly recalls, is in arrears regarding a recent loan on a race at the local trottery.

Hot and cold, opposites attract, enough forgiveness for one day. Our forgiven friend is in no mood to diffuse the Higher Law. A secret rankling, a residue of anger, the tingling of a hand lately caught in the till drawer. The steward minces no words. He grabs the meagre scullion by the throat: Pay up, scurvy fellow! Think you not I know your horse came in?

A reversal of roles, a kind of nightmarish continuity. Another servant-master scene. The stable boy kneels, he repeats word for word the plaint so lately on the lips of the cornered accountant. "All I ask is a few more days, you'll have your money . . . ."

But no mercy. Mercy is for the very rich; our friend is only so-so rich.

Besides, there's a question of principle here. If I go around forgiving every two-bit crook in sight, what's to become of law and order and gratitude; and religion, even?

He goes on throttling. In good conscience. Indeed he owes it to faith and family to go on throttling.

And he all but chokes the life out of this all but former servant. It's not the money, it's the principle of the thing!

The other servants come on the run, the hubbub is terrific.

They halt matters, just in time. They pull the two apart, and shake some life back into the dimunitive delinquent.

Then the servants march into their lord and master, with this sad tale of the unforgiving servant, this fervent upholder of virtue, this throttler of small fry.

Most of them seem to be ignorant of the earlier blowout; everything has happened too fast. They don't like to see a little fellow, whose only crime is that he studies the racing forms and now and again lays a few bucks on a fast or slow horse, but is after all quite a decent chap, all but killed.

Lord and master, they say, that steward of yours has just finished nearly offing one of our fellow servants. We know he's very high on your pay scale, but still. You should have seen it. He was really choking him to death. And all for the matter of a few bucks, when as we understand things, this chief steward rakes in plenty from here and there, and where

101

he gets his capital outlay no one seems to know, but don't think we don't have ideas . . . Anyway we thought you should know. That stable boy who got in the way of your steward, never hurt a horse tick, but you should have seen him white as flour and gasping for breath. We had to hold him upside down and jiggle him around just to get him going again.

And as if all this wasn't enough, your steward went off and phoned the cops who were at the front door in no time flat. And our little fellow servant is at present languishing in the slammer until he pays up. Now how can anyone in the slammer pay up? It just doesn't make any sense.

By now their lord and master was on the near edge of apoplexy. His eyes stood out from his head, he was red as an unburped baby. Go get him, bring him in here, was all he could roar.

You know the rest. This sort of conduct isn't tolerated in the kingdom, even in the kingdom of the dollar. And the lord and master of the kingdom of the dollar may not resemble the lord of heaven as closely as we wish; but he knows when he's been had. That's why he yelled out, Payola's one thing, forgiveness another. Bring him in!

And our forgiven friend, that master of the double standard, gold and silver, cringe and throttle, finds himself shortly tossed into durance vile, debtor's prison to be exact.

Now as to the moral of all this: the only crime that is not forgiven, is the crime of not forgiving.

In this does the billionaire of this world, a not totally admirable character, resemble the father of all.

The story began, you note, with a kind of socratic exchange: How often should I forgive?

Some Christians might be inclined to come down hard on Peter's question — especially if the question of forgiveness hasn't occurred to them as a serious question at all. But as to Peter, doesn't he show a regrettable tendency to keep scores, tote up gains and losses, times forgiven, times left hanging, scores settled? And shouldn't we Christians be above all that?

Maybe we should be. Maybe though, we shouldn't be

above the Lord, who is inclined to take Peter seriously, to the point of telling a partly humorous, totally serious story of divine forgiveness and human ironheartedness.

And then there are those haunting words from the cross, words, which we will never quite explain away: Father forgive them.

In sum, it seems to me there is no way of taking the Lord seriously without taking Peter seriously. Because his question goes to the heart of the Christian witness, and because the Lord's response is one of his most perplexing, dismaying words in the whole testament.

On the first point, volumes have been written; and, infinitely more troubling, much blood split. From the shedding of the blood of Abel to the death of Stephen Biko, what a testimony of non-violent love both preceded the Lord's coming, and was impelled by his example!

Indeed when one gives thought to the matter, what else has Christianity to offer the world? It seems to me that every other glory, every historic contribution, from the so called triumphs of the middle ages, the fierce dynamism, the voyages, the vanishing frontiers, the evangelising of the tribes of the earth — all is ambiguous, stained with crime, cupidity, blood-letting. How few have shown forth the forgiving non-violent love of the Savior! And but for the few who have, what continuity could we claim today with the spirit of the Savior? We are shamed; for the most part, we have wasted our birthright.

As to the Lord's story, it exceeds his accustomed modesty. Imagine. Millions of shekels are involved, massive fraud, implying a vastly greater fortune to "borrow" from; the fortune of creation itself, a kind of cosmic gross product. And as to forgiveness, the Lord waxes equally flamboyant; the sky is the limit.

Thus he challenges us. Name the most outrageous crime conceivable (against property). Whatever the amount embezzled, lifted, stolen, I counsel forgiveness. In forgiving, let us be immodest; indeed, let us not raise obstacles to the free flow of the forgiving spirit in comparison with which the larceny and rip off of the material universe itself is to be thought of as — precisely nothing.

You inform me, said the king, that certain shady elements have made off with the World Trade Towers, occupied the Brooklyn Bridge and pocketed the tolls; have hijacked the wonders of the Metropolitan Museum, have ransacked Bloomingdales; and at present are occupied in dismembering the Cloisters and shipping that marvel, stone by stone, to Saudi Arabia.

You are vastly disturbed at all this; you come to me, seeking a fitting Christian response.

Let me, at risk of redundancy, repeat a word of my son; seventy times seventy times. Allow me to paraphrase him. If they come for the Brooklyn Bridge, give them two others; the Manhattan and the George Washington. If they covet the spoils of the Metropolitan Museum, throw in freely the Whitney and the Museum of Modern Art. Heap coals of fire, pour the bullion of Fort Knox on their heads. Walk a second mile with the thieves. If they covet your sheared nutria coat, toss in the camel's hair and the Gucci shoes. After all, your cupidity has assembled all these; are you to deny to others what is ill gotten in yourself? And if questions of larceny are seriously pursued, who of you will stand guiltless?

Still, questions arise. What of good sense and moderation, even in such admittedly lofty matters? And what about the encouragement of criminal tendencies, by this will of putting up with literally any onslaught? What about embezzlers and muggers and pickpockets? And what about a sensible love of possessions that enhance our lives? And please describe for us a suitable attitude toward material things, when one wishes to provide sensibly for the welfare of children or the elderly or sick?

And so on. And so on.

It must be clear, our story of the king and the thieving steward takes up not one of these perplexing questions. And on purpose; for like any good story, this one has only a single point to make. Forgive. There are nuances however, and implications. All vexations and niceties and footnotes to the matter of forgiveness, can be settled without the presence of Christ. These are after all, worldly matters, well within the competence of people of the world. There is no pressing need for a divine one, to settle these questions. But in one area, there is indeed a need that surpasses all human resources, that implies so improbable an event as the crucifixion of God. It is the matter of forgiveness.

Forgive, they say, and forget. But they forget that "forgetting" in this sequence, is redundant. Forgiveness is forgetting.

What is truly forgiven is regarded as if it had never been. A radical erasure of the offense. But more; a new beginning.

Can we forgive our God this kind of forgiveness? Many, it would seem, can not. They demand a God who punishes their inability to accept forgiveness. They are at peace only with a God who is at war with them. Thus they welcome to their breast, the killing weapons of the god of nations. And the cycle of damnation is very nearly closed. The god of death has killed them. They are now his prey.

Every mode of conduct recommended by Jesus, is first verified, tested, in his own soul. The method is sublime, generous; but it has its rigor too. It invites us not merely to be "good", but to be godlike.

There is trouble here. The invitation, and the ikon, are unsettling in the extreme. Who wants to resemble a God who so little resembles us? Cosmetic surgery isn't called for, but death and rebirth. So we bungle along. Idols are our main love. Resembling them is called a vocation. And nothing much happens — in us, or in the world.

The "forgetting" aspect of forgiving is at least as difficult as the "remembering" aspect of the eucharist. Which is to say, without forgiveness, there can be no remembering, no healing. There is only dismembering. The old order stands intact, which is the order of malice and death and anger and war on life. But of newness, nothing. And the eucharist is pure disarray, anomie, a shambles.

We would like to limit the area of forgiveness; one to one, a psychological impasse. Or ease it, with a professional smile, into our tete-a-tetes, where cover up and politesse are the name of the game. Far off the gospel track, it goes without saying.

Who has given serious thought to the mandate of Jesus, as it touches on the crimes of the nations, on war? At this point, the churches turn to stone. They give up on the gospel as they give up on the citizens; indeed, the acts are one act, one betrayal.

And at precisely this point, somberly and seriously, the vocation of the Christian begins; insofar as we will admit that we have a vocation at all. It is a call to radical forgiveness — that is to say, to non-violence, to absolute non-cooperation with murder. The call comes on a most unlikely occasion; just when the gospel is being jettisoned into a sea of wrath by the inert gesture of clerics. The Christian is called to dive into that fire, to rescue the word of life, at cost of his own life, if required. (It will sometimes be required.)

Let us admit that we are as unprepared for all this as was the least and last of the Lord's hearers, on the day he first proclaimed his difficult (difficult? say, impossible) word.

But the word of forgiveness cannot be understood, if its ambit is limited to, let us say, crimes against property. This would be sheer nonsense; I have suggested the humorous treatment God gives such ideas, the contempt with which he regards the shifts and wrangles that break out when the Mafia is a ruling metaphor and method.

No, the point of forgiveness is something more; otherwise the gospel curls up at the hearth of the culture, another fat cat.

The modern state's stated response to the gospel, is murder, pure and simple. Kill, do not forgive. At such a point, the state not only shows its true face. (It has always shown its true face.) But at such a point (which can be verified in any or every moment of modern life) the immoral state confronts the believing citizen with the only crisis faith is likely to encounter today. The state even becomes an occasion of awakening the Christian to his true vocation.

How that vocation is swallowed whole in the iron jaws of Mars, how citizen-believers (citizens first, believers maybe) disappear without a cry into that maw, is the story of most of us, throughout most of history. All our wars are Christian wars, to paraphrase the sublime Chesterton. A statement which is not necessarily cynical. But what it underscores, all but celebrates, is the foolishness, the radical impossibility, of the Lord's command. It reassures, in a strange way. Without God, one cannot be godlike. One can only be bestial, in a way far beneath the conduct of beasts.

This is our history, granted. This is not our destiny. Consult the sermon on the mount.

Or perhaps it is our destiny. Then let us leave off this chatter, make our main study the U.S. Marines Handbook, jettison the gospel. And enlist in America.

But at least, let us leave behind this tawdry, no person land, the "modern church", where everything is a kind of twilight duplicity, alienation, anomie, — and let us strike out, in uniform, weapons on the alert, on the prowl with the Beast. There are children out there, to be murdered. There are hospitals to be bombed. There are properties to be protected at gunpoint, people to be eliminated, prisoners to be interrogated under torture, all the ordinary "business" of the modern state to be pushed. There is good American citizenship to be verified. By us.

If such talk seems unutterably hideous, consider the last fifteen years, and what was required and fullfilled, by good American youths on the bodies of Vietnamese people. Consider what was acceded to, in silence, by most of us. And what was blessed, approved, or ignored by the churches.

The swaddling and psychologizing of life today is not only degrading, it is also, biblically speaking, deviant. How strange it is that a people who shed human feeling in order to wage a hideous war, find that their feelings are now sacrosanct, that in fact psychology is their mainstay in coping with post war America. And that in the process, their "needs" are elevated to a rarified, sanctified consumerism. On the other hand, such a stern, publicly crucial reality as biblical forgiveness, is made into a muttering commerce between casualties. In such wise, we are less and less able to be ourselves, or to become ourselves; publicly alert, responsible, morally conscious. We are no longer accorded the dubious dignity of citizens. We are a nation of clients, patients, malingerers.

It seems as though psychology, and a psychologized church, are the newest enlistees of Big Brother. They present him with a nursery of children, or a city morgue packed with the dead; or a casualty ward of broken spirits, victims of cold and hot war on the soul. This is a triumph of death, and the death of the gospel. For the dead can neither be violent or non-violent; they are the perfect expression of silent citizenry.

And as modern war requires less and less the services of trained killers, a morally hyped, skinless citizenry is more and more needed. Wind the people up in a tangled knot of emotional quackery, ethical helplessness, tears, conniptions, tantrums — and let the state go about its business. Which is war. Trust the state. Deal with your own problems, first and last. Ten years on the couch is a good investment. Thus the psychologists and the imperium offer severally their shoddy circuses and stale bread, in cahoots, more or less consciously.

## And Lead Us Not Into
## Temptation, but Deliver Us from Evil

("Do not bring us to the testing, but keep us safe from the
evil one." [Today's English Version.] "And do not put us to
the test, but save us from the evil one." [Jerusalem Bible.])

Yet God did precisely this to his son: brought him to hard
testing; put him to the test. In the desert, in the garden of
Gethsemane.

Are we asking to be spared the things Jesus endured? Let us
not say yes too easily. For that matter, let us not say no too
easily.

The two testings, the first at the start of his public life, the
other toward the end, seem to me quite different, and require
separate treatment. The first is a kind of socratic testing;
"does this person know who he is?" One's prior life is put in
question, everything suddenly is clouded and unsure. The desert offers a test proper to youth, a kind of rite of passage. Is
one merely going over the same ground as one's parents,
tracked by their life, overshadowed, haunted?

But the testing also has a subtler aspect. What indeed is
Jesus to do, when the symbolic heroes, the nobles and saints
of the past are called up, shades at a banquet? Are they summoned to bless, verify, witness to this wonder worker, kingly
one, liberator? Indeed, the desert is no banquet, but the great
eyed ghosts are there. Is this newcomer not their blood brother, called to be like them, to do the deeds of Moses, David,
the messiah?

He is to be like them, of course. And he is to be unlike them.

If he were totally unlike them, he would lose the grace of continuity that in fact bound him, soul and body, to the history of his people. In certain crucial respects, he must be, is called to be, the new David, the new Moses, the awaited messiah. In a manner of speaking, he must turn stones to bread and exert moral dominion and be a striking sign of God's love.

Still, he must be himself. He must take his own direction, follow his own star. He must surpass and even scandalize. He cannot be a mere image of his human ancestry . . .

The tempter smiles from the mirror of creation. He would have Jesus walk into the mirror, and be absorbed there.

Jesus looks long and steadily. He takes the tempter seriously. But what he sees is not a truthful image of himself. Not even a truthful image of his ancestors. He sees only the blasphemous beckoning smile. Be like me, for I am god.

Jesus breaks the mirror with a blow, and turns away.

It is not these proffers (kingship, liberator, messiah) that make the desert temptation what it is, a moment of danger and deflection. After all, Jesus will perform each of the acts stipulated, miraculous, awesome as they are. He will perform them simply, matter of factly; no great matter. Walking on water, multiplying bread, even summoning the dead to life. And he himself will rise from the dead.

All this, but with a difference.

His acts will be godlike. As proposed to him, they are satanic.

Satanic, divine, what is this difference?

He is tempted to abandon the ruling metaphor of his existence: Son/Father. But listen to Satan: "I have another version of things. Let these great deeds stand by themselves, let your life stand by itself. Finish this utter mutuality, this self emptying, this voiding of ego, the free flow of your power and the father's . . .

112

"Let me be precise, satanic. I am not urging you to refer your deeds to Satan, to give me the glory, instead of to the father. I am urging you to be like me. This is, to refer your miracles to yourself. To say in effect; it all starts here, it all ends here, it is all mine.

"You see I am not being mephistophelean. Only satanic. I am not urging a pact between you and me, or bartering for your soul. Indeed, you have only to nod, to accede, and I disappear forever.

"Come, test my altruism. Let your appearance on the human scene be my signal to disappear . . . ."

We know from the book of Revelation that the church will be tempted to play Satan. We have seen the temptation acted out in our time. When the church, like the imperial state, announces; "all power is mine." The words are often translated today; "structures first, people second". At that point, church and state coincide in fact. And the gospel is extinguished.

"I will keep you from the hour of trial, which is coming on the whole earth, to try those who dwell upon the earth." (Rev. 3, 10) "And if those days had not been shortened, no human being would be saved; but for the sake of the elect, those days will be shortened." (Mt. 24, 23)

Today, the conjunction of mad weaponry and madder minds, has given a horrid urgency to the "testing" spoken of in our prayer.

The trouble is, that the "great trouble" has not come upon us, it has rather been inflicted by us, and the act of killing places the killer at a disadvantage; he is blind to the suffering he has brought to pass. Americans have traveled to Hiroshima on pilgrimages of expiation. Others went south to Selma or Birmingham during the '60's, took part in freedom rides, shared the dangers and violence inflicted on the blacks. And Willy Brandt knelt at Dachau, before the incinerators. Someday it is conceivable even that an American president will kneel in the streets of Hanoi, in expiation of the crimes of Kennedy, Johnson and Nixon.

Thinking of such moments, we feel as though time has stopped; indeed that our hearts had stopped beating. A time of unprecedented suffering, tribulation, then a moment of truth. Indeed, the end of a world, the end of the old world of inevitable multiplied violence and cheap death. And at least an inkling of a new world; in which murder will not be entirely legal and beyond accounting.

The "time of testing" is not to be thought of merely as a time of arbitrary upheavals in nature. The Christians and Jews of Jesus' time had something else in mind; the lawless arm of an occupying power. The suffering when it fell, was in no sense an "act of God." It was a deliberate imperial arrangement, an extermination policy, pure and simple.

And today, if the "time of testing" is shortened due to the prayers of the saints, surely it is implied that the saints have had no part in creating so hideous a time. Unfortunately for us, we are back in an old theme; that of resistance to the lawless state.

It is arguable (many Jews argue it passionately) that a debased Christianity created Hitler and his horrors. At least it could be said that a climate of silence in a so-called Christian country created a vacuum into which racist madness could move like a tainted arrow. It is similarly arguable that only a tainted Christianity could create the neutron bomb. At least, again, an atmosphere of sheeplike quasi-religious complicity so enveloped the cold war years, that it justified a hideous crusade against "the enemy"; who as time went on, became all-seeing, all-powerful. The enemy was largely self-created. Christianity, as they say, demands a crusade.

The end of a culture or a civilization or a political structure is certainly not the end of the world. True enough; but too simple to describe our own situation. Now we have a culture (we are a culture) capable of bringing down the world. Apocalyptic anger and the neutron bomb.

The moral pollution of the nuclear age stops all our clocks. As the explosion stopped the clocks of Hiroshima, forever. Now we are in twilight, the "silva oscura" of Dante. It is crucial that we not simply wander there, bereft of land marks. Let us learn to live in the darkness, taking one step at a time, modestly, as befits those who would not light their way by brimstone and bombs.

Taking all this in account — the holocaust, Hiroshima, Vietnam, ourselves. What have we learned, what have we unlearned? Are we grown more acute, adult, sacrificial, patient, giving? And above all perhaps — modest? Certainly we are not to play god; this is precisely the sin of our leadership, in church and state. Something more biblical and indeed more difficult is required: to be human. This is the time of testing; a price lies on the head of one who would be human.

The plea for deliverance implies two truths; each of them runs strongly counter to current myths.

The first truth: there is an evil to be delivered from. The truth counters the myth of the people of God, the people of the covenant, the people of providence. How weary one grows of such ego stroking, in churches, in public! The second truth is that we cannot, by hook, crook, bomb, diplomacy, threat, curse, incantation, gross national product, angel or demon, bell, book or lighted candle — we cannot deliver ourselves. We cannot save ourselves. No inspired or demonic or religious or democratic or marxist or maoist misuse or good use of the world or of our own lives, can bring us ease. Discontent, exasperation, the age of anxiety. We are stuck. We are stuck where we are. We are in this morass of good intentions and bad conduct, of self deception and the high art of public crime. The good that we would do, we do not do.

It is a very old story. But its being old does not make it currently influential. Quite the contrary. Something called "scientific progress", something called "psychiatric breakthrough" has gotten powerfully in the way of the truth. We are surely as weak and foolish as our forebears; but we are deprived of the self knowledge of a tradition. We would like to amend the text of Paul, to wipe out its searching and fruitful contradictions. Here is our announcement to the world (and to our former God): The good that we would do, behold how splendidly we do it. The evil that we would avoid, behold how resolutely we avoid it.

This is not merely nonsense, flying in the face of the truth; it is pernicious nonsense. Would that the self deception stopped with us. But it catapults us into the world, to rain death down on peoples who cannot, even under the harshest duress, accept our version of reality.

The opposite of a cry for deliverance is the secular covenant. The cry for deliverance is the heart of the biblical covenant. Shall we cry out, or shall we create victims who cry out? (But we are also the victims.) The testing is the blessing. But if there is no testing, there is only a curse. Our curse is that the testing is done elsewhere; always elsewhere. Nuclear testing. Testing of germ warfare; soon, neutron bomb testing. It is always a mechanism; it is always destructive; it is always on someone else's turf or flesh. We "do" the testing, we inflict it. Thus we play God and escape the human condition. But not forever.

What strikes one about our Christianity is its paltriness. What strikes one about America is its gigantism. In New York, Catholic authorities are presently heating up for a gay witch hunt. The big guns are smoking, a macho priest, dressed to kill, appears on TV. He presents, with that deadly seriousness which only bad faith can summon, the dangers to "our children", if these sinister stalkers are allowed their civil rights. It is all a bit like an elephant safari setting out against grey mice.

Meantime, if a hydrogen bomb were fitted out with a cockpit, a Cardinal would probably ride the prototype aloft, scattering a fallout of blessings. My bomb, right or wrong. The paltries have joined the gigantics. Their antics are outrageously similar.

The shortening of the time of testing is due, the Lord says, to the prayer of the saints. In view of these prayers, under the hypothesis of those prayers. Those prayers are taken into account. Otherwise, all would perish. We see how seriously God takes prayer; including the Lord's Prayer. Apart from such prayers, he would lose patience with your crimes. In a sense that quite escapes common sense, his patience is our testing. And our salvation.

Common forms of testing in the imperial state, for those citizens who choose to be believers (not who wish to be "also" believers, which is the usual priority, but believers pure and simple) might take the following forms:

— Anguish and depression of the spirit, knowing that one is bound not to be listened to, except by a few. But never by those in the cockpit.

— The difficult balance between leveling off and living at white heat. In the first, one merely enlists in the age; as one joins the armed forces, or the church. It is all a blunting and silencing. In the second, one becomes merely fantastic or nostalgic; after one big flare, one recedes into the shadows, into folklore. Not a very nourishing diet.

— The omnipresence of morbid religion. Which is to say, almost any religion on the market today. Invariably, these cure alls either tiptoe around the bible, or close it with a bang, or pervert it into a history of silly putty figurines. Or, because one must believe in something (and must call the belief sacred because we have invented it) we laboriously write our own bible. A genesis that creates nothing. An exodus that goes no where. A book of laws that nails the heart to a wall. Prophets who are vain or virulent. A secular messiah who damns the right and blesses wrong. A wisdom literature that is pure folly. And then a "new testament"; a secular covenant with America; astrology, drug confabulation, cupidity, political opportunism. The sermon on the mount, inside out. And finally, an apocryphal apocalypse; author, Herman Kahn.

Thus in sum, the American anti-bible. It is as native to the culture as the Marines Handbook, out of which we drew the recipe in 1968 for home cooked napalm.

— Anomie. The death of common symbols, ways of seeing and telling.

— The Catholic principle, rampant. i.e., magic. The wickedness or stoniness of our hearts makes no difference; Jesus "works through all that."

— The Protestant principle, rampant; i.e., inwardness unrelieved. The criterion of genuine worship is my "feeling" about worship.

— Jargon. Noise. The explorers have gone off to Samarkand, with empty sacks, to capture and bring back alive, spoils of silence. But they never returned. Stories drifted back; they had fallen through a crevasse in the upper reaches of the Himalayas. O the perils of that expedition! And instead of silence, we gained — precisely nothing. Well, no doubt about it, we must send out another expedition . . . .

— Shrinkage. In a slang sense; the world inert, on couches, talking to mechanical SONYs. In a more literal sense, the search, seldom undertaken, rarely successful, for a fulcrum that will move the world. A fulcrum that, wonder of wonders, will move ourselves.

## An Afterword

I reflect on this prayer, and on the one who offered its words and phrases to us, with his own lips. And my heart is filled with wonderment. It seems to me that we might expect any benefit, any surprise, from a God who will teach us to pray. We might even hope that such a God will die for us.

I work at a hospital for the dying, as a kind of orderly-at-large. The place is like an air lifted building, ever so gently taken up, put down just as gently, somewhere out of this time and place. The hospital does not seem to exist in New York City at all. The river goes swiftly by, and the streams of traffic. Not signs of presence, but a kind of ghostly charade. The dying look out on the river of time, the river of the living, from the wheelchairs and beds. They look out as though from an air ship or another planet. They watch it all go by. Their look is detached and level; now and again it is ironic. All this motion, restlessness, pursuit, agitation, has lost nearly all meaning. They have let it all go.

I have never seen a door close, even the door of prison, with quite the finality with which these doors shut. Everything that makes the city seductive, exciting, various, a fireworks, a shadow box of marvels, — here it is muted, slowed. Everything that makes the city a horror, a mad mix of contention, sweat, exasperation, cupidity, furor, — all is exorcised.

The exorcism is a sweat box, a threshing floor, a double millstone, a crucible. It is called death. Here the dying grow skilled in the art of dying. And those like myself, a bit short of that skill, that moment, may yet learn, if we are apt at learning anything.

The hospital is out of our time zone; out of any time zone. This is another source of trouble for awhile, as one slowly turns his clocks right. No one hurries here, there are few emergencies, no time is lost, no running after buses, no speeding through streets, no beating lights, no vexation at late this or delayed that. No part in a mechanism that functions in any case, badly. Here you wait, everyone waits. You are here on a project that is all but unheard of in the city. You are here to serve. It is, believe it or not, a far lesser dignity than being served.

Sometimes this image occurs to me. I am accompanying a sick person to the office of a renowned mysterious surgeon. Both of us sit and wait. Then a door opens, a voice says; next please. My friend goes in alone. He has met the healer death. He is in better hands than I, or this world, can offer.

Day by day in the savage New York winter, I set down these reflections. On Thursdays I travel to the hospital. It seems important to me in an obscure way, to health of spirit and body, to go there. For the hospital is quite simply a place where the Lord's prayer can be said with all one's heart. It is not merely urgency and pain that pierce one to the quick. It is something more. The prayer which elsewhere is clouded or diluted by the vile humors of the world, is uttered in a kind of purity and suspension. Any day will crack the fragile glass. Any day will rend the veil. And does. The walls are fragile, delicate as a drinking glass. The right note is struck, the glass is shattered.

There are places where death is the main and repeated event. Our world has multiplied them beyond measure. There are slums which beggar description; prisons which snuff the lives of the hardiest. And then the spectaculars; the smoking pits and pockmarks of Hanoi and Dresden and Hiroshima.

The hospital is another place of death. Death is the main event. But when I think of this hospital and of those who pray and work and die there, I think of the simplicity and naturalness of a faith which is in its rightful setting.

122

In one sense, the hospital is out of this world. It exists apart from all who serve appetite, Mammon, war, hatred, all our idols. In another sense, perhaps the more precious one, the hospital is planted deep in this world. Its clients are the urban poor, the castaways, the lost and forgotten and unwanted. Here they are at length welcome, to live as long and decently as they might, to die when they must or choose.

Meantime: a sense of meantime: of lives filled to bursting, not with hideous invading growths, but with the teeming life of seed, vats, harvests.

A short step separates the dying from all their longing and laurels. But to take that step! It is physically and morally unlikely. They must step out on turbulent waters, leave the vessel behind. They are bedridden, hopelessly, and their healing demands that they lurch upright, take a first step. They cannot. And yet they must. This is the dilemma; it may be the deliverance. One by one, the impossible occurs. One by one, they walk away from us. Into — what? I think of the tearing of that veil, the breaking of that glass. The dying cease to petition the Lord, in the act of petition. Everything is suddenly granted. The text of the prayer is torn up and tossed to high heaven. Each laborious bloodstained tear marked petition ignites in midair, a hymn, a glory.

Imagine the sudden translation, physically, literally, of that prayer petition.

*Our father, we are in heaven, your name is hallowed. Your kingdom has come.*
*All earth is now heaven, your will is our own.*
*Thank you for that daily bread. It was very good.*
*Thank you for forgiving us. We have also forgiven others.*
*And thank you for shortening the time of testing.*
*And for this deliverance.*
*Amen. Alleluia.*